PENGUIN BOOKS
WHERE ON EARTH AM I?

Jug Suraiya is a columnist, and an associate editor with the
Times of India. He is the author of several books.

Where on Earth Am I?

Confusions of a Travelling Man

JUG SURAIYA

PENGUIN BOOKS

Penguin Books India (P) Ltd, 11 Community Centre, Panchsheel Park, New Delhi 110 017, India
Penguin Books Ltd, 80 Strand, London WC2R 0RL, UK
Penguin Group (USA) Inc., 375 Hudson Street, New York, NY 10014, USA
Penguin Books Australia Ltd, 250 Camberwell Road, Camberwell, Victoria 3124, Australia
Penguin Books Canada Ltd, 10 Alcorn Avenue, Suite 300, Toronto, Ontario, M4V 3B2, Canada
Penguin Group (NZ), cnr Airborne and Rosedale Roads, Albany, Auckland 1310, New Zealand
Penguin Books (South Africa) (Pty) Ltd, 24 Sturdee Avenue, Rosebank 2196, South Africa

First published by Penguin Books India 2004
Copyright © Jug Suraiya 2004

All rights reserved

10 9 8 7 6 5 4 3 2 1

Typeset in Sabon by S.R. Enterprises, New Delhi
Printed at Pauls Press, New Delhi

To Bunny,
who always manages to find me,
even when I don't know where I am.

WE SHALL NOT CEASE FROM EXPLORATION
AND THE END OF ALL OUR EXPLORING
WILL BE TO ARRIVE WHERE WE STARTED
AND KNOW THE PLACE FOR THE FIRST TIME

—T.S. ELIOT

Contents

Preface

'Why on earth do we travel?' Many people have asked this question. And I think that there are as many answers to it as there are travellers.

I was a traveller long before I knew I was. As a young boy in Calcutta, I would walk along the streets and avenues and bylanes of the city. I would pass decaying mansions, elegant bungalows set in shaded gardens, teeming tenements. As I walked by, I would look in through open windows, catching stray glimpses of what was within: A naked light bulb; a crystal chandelier; a man in a singlet sitting at a table, lost in thought and cigarette smoke; a child holding a headless doll; a beautiful woman looking at her face in the mirror. I would invent stories about the people who lived there, and what my life would have been like if I had been one of them. No, I wasn't a voyeur, a word I had never heard of at the time. I was just a storyteller recounting to myself the many narratives that might have been me.

Physicists say that the universe we inhabit is only one in an infinite series of universes, not out there in distant space, but only a heartbeat away from us in a different dimension. Each time we open a door, pick up a book, start a conversation, we give rise to a countless progression of universes where we left the door shut, picked up not this but some other book, stayed silent rather than spoke. The world we know is only one of an infinitude of narratives of which, unaware, we are a part. I would like to think that what we call travel is a faint echo of that never-ending story of which we are both the narrators and the subjects.

This collection of travel writing spans almost thirty years and several continents, from Castro's Cuba to post-perestroika Russia, from Chinese-ruled Tibet to death-haunted Argentina. Some of the pieces are in a lighter vein, others are more serious. They have one thing in common. They are all seen through the eyes of a boy walking the long-ago streets of Calcutta, wondering what story about himself the next open window would reveal.

HOME

Nagaland Encounter

In 1974, at the height of the insurgency, I toured Nagaland for eight days as a feature writer for the Calcutta-based Junior Statesman (JS) *magazine. I was accompanied by Teki, the* JS *photographer.*

I haven't been to Nagaland since. But from occasional media reports it seems that though hostilities have ebbed, the Naga situation remains basically what it was almost thirty years ago. In our national monomania about Kashmir, we appear to have forgotten Nagaland, and indeed the whole of the north-east.

Unfortunately for them, the Nagas can't similarly forget themselves. What is the future of the Nagas? I don't pretend to know. The account of my Nagaland journey ends with a song of peace composed by a student. Today, twenty-nine years after I first read them, the words of the song remain written on the wind.

At the one-and-a-half shacks that constitute the terminal office at Dimapur airport, a flyblown tourist poster said: 'Welcome to Nagaland'. Our shawl-clad tourist officer footnoted, 'Please don't worry. You won't get shot at.' And, with a smile of reassurance that didn't quite communicate itself, he steered Teki and me to the waiting jeep.

We soon left the gritty border town of Dimapur and the plains behind, and began the long, winding climb to Kohima, the 4800-foot-high capital. The road wound through hills explosive with subtropical lushness, windmilled with banana fronds and wistful with bamboo. The occasional knoll or slope was scrubbed bare of vegetation to accommodate an army post—an encircling bristle of pointed bamboo staves, a dun mud wall, men with casual guns and careful enamel mugs of tea.

The first preconceived notion to get shot down was the schedule. Our jeep broke down. Fortunately, it was just outside a small township, Ghaspani, thirty-nine kilometres from Kohima. We waited at Ghaspani for a bus, a lift, a minor miracle. It was a tiny place, a handful of corrugated-tin-roofed buildings strung together by the road and backed by vegetable patches. Four young men in red-and-black-and green Angami shawls played a clamorous game of carrom on the street, the board atop an old tar barrel. The few shops sold overpriced cigarettes and soggy biscuits. Pigs rooted around in grunting perambulation, and squawking chickens scuttled out of the way of the sporadic traffic—lorries laden with cement sacks and pipes, and a solitary army patrol. Two buses from Dimapur, bound for Kohima, wheezed by, but it was no go; there were no seats. The local motor workshop had confirmed our worst suspicions regarding our jeep, and our guide, unduly contrite, coaxed us to a nearby verandah. For Teki and me it was our first taste of Naga hospitality. Though we had wandered into the house uninvited, cane chairs and mugs of tea were swiftly produced with a smiling insistence which brooked no demurral. In the frugally furnished room behind, we caught sight of a colourful *JS* fashion-spread. Through an interpreter who spoke Nagamese (the pidgin Assamese which intercommunicates between Nagaland's sixteen major and very different dialects) we asked our host if anyone in his family read the magazine. No, he replied, but we like the pictures.

Just then a speeding jeep screeched to a halt outside. A young man in a white hat and shorts leapt out and our guide broke into vociferous greetings. They pumped each other's hands warmly, discovered that each wasn't quite who the other had thought he was, but they had a common distant cousin anyway, so what difference did it make? This is one of the lovely things about living in a state with a population of a little over five lakhs. You either know everyone already or, if you don't, you feel you should, which makes it fine anyway.

Dumping luggage and ourselves in the back of the jeep we roared off—Kohima or bust. At several hair-raising moments during the ride, I thought it would be the latter. For the driver, a cheerful eighteen-year-old with a white hat identical to his boss's, drove with the vigorous recklessness of a truant charioteer from *Ben-Hur*. In between sudden tugs of centrifugal and centripetal forces we discovered that the young man who had offered us the lift was a government vet just returning from a six-week study-cum-work stint in Shillong. Nagaland's economy is almost totally based on agriculture and its ancillaries, and the study of field sciences such as animal husbandry and forestry is officially encouraged, students receiving a government scholarship of Rs 175 per month.

We saw Kohima long before we got to it. The white sprinkle on the distant green became colonies, houses, tin roofs, walls, windows, and we were climbing through the new residential suburbs and into the market area where, in the early evening, it seemed the entire 23,000-plus population of Kohima had congregated, calling out to each other and us as we passed.

The jeep deposited us at the half-finished MLA Hostel, just below the Kohima Assembly, and we shoved our luggage into our room. An hour later, dark and cold outside by now, we were huddled around a table in a minuscule coffee shop, a large espresso machine making hissing noises in a corner in counterpoint to the allegro of our debate with a group of young locals.

In urban Nagaland, particularly in Kohima, where you often cannot see the 'cracy' for the various 'bureaus', the bread and butter, or dal and rice, of any conversational feast is politics.

Everyone talks politics, including those who keep insisting that they dislike politics and then adduce political reasons for their dislike. The root cause of this over-sensitized political consciousness is what has nationally and internationally come to be known as 'the Naga situation'. After over two decades of often sensational and sometimes biased press reportage, the broadcast of contradictory political statements, and a tragic chain reaction of violence and counter-violence, this 'situation' has attained the phantasmagoric complexity of a nightmare come true. There are no 'facts' to the case, no hard, clear outlines, just a shimmering haze of rumours, grapevine gossip, myths, and interpretations.

Even the service in the tiny coffee bar seemed to have been infected with the endemic unreality, for though we had ordered espresso, plates of fried eggs mysteriously appeared, and disappeared, and a twenty-one-year-old Naga at our table said impassionedly, 'We talk, talk, talk all the effing time, and no one really knows what is happening. Say an incidence takes place—a raid, a meeting—and you ask ten people to tell you what happened. The first eight will probably say they don't know. The ninth will tell you for sure just what happened. And the tenth will just as confidently say exactly the opposite.'

One of the young men in the coffee shop was Ricky Medom, a second-year pre-university student—shoulder-length hair, flared trousers, an interest in pop music—whose father was a member of the Nagaland Public Service Commission and whose uncles were both 'undergrounds', one the 'underground home minister' and the other 'General' Thinouselie who was being trained by the Pakistani army and was captured during the Bangladesh operations. The intangible, omnipresent 'underground' cuts across social, tribal, and even family lines. Ricky's self-admitted ambition was to join the Indian Administrative Service. Ricky's family is far from being an exception. There are, literally, hundreds of such families, split down the centre by an intangible divide. To make things more bewildering, even these strange patterns are not constant but often change kaleidoscopically as 'undergrounds' come above ground, and those who were above sometimes go under, in a shifting, intricate weave as nimble as the craft which looms

the colourful, enveloping Naga shawls. The talk was politics
and continued late into the night, blue-hazed with cigarette
smoke and sparked with controversy.

Adda, as Teki and I discovered that night, is as popular a
pastime in Nagaland as anywhere else in India. Almost
invariably at these sessions the mythically perfect
'underground' rebel is eulogized in tales of heroic exploits.
There are wild and woolly stories aplenty. Of how a company
of troops was made to surrender, the soldiers magnanimously
spared but stripped naked and sent back to camp with a
'safe conduct' letter from the 'underground' leader to 'protect'
them on their way. Or the time when a lone 'underground',
sitting in a tavern, was jumped by two 'Armies' and how, in
the twinkling of a trigger, he had overturned the table and
shot them both dead (all 'undergrounds', incidentally, are
legendarily expert marksmen).

Heroines too have their share of glory. Like the girl who
seduced an officer in order to filch his Sten gun for the
'underground' cause. The rebels are also supposedly possessed
of devious intelligence which they use in psychological tactics,
staging ambushes near neutral or pro-government villages
so that the resultant punitive measures imposed in the area
by the authorities will cause the villagers to swing towards
the 'underground'.

Few politically sophisticated people believe these stories.
But the anecdotes, vigorously flavoured with adventure and
salty humour, have gained a broad popularity, and appeal to
the Nagas' innate sense of empathy with the underdog, the
fighter who takes on all odds (J.P. Narayan, for example,
figures often and favourably in conversation). But more than
all this, is the feeling of ethnic oneness. As a young ex-student
leader put it, 'They might be misguided but they are still
patriots. In the end, we are all Nagas.'

The next morning, Kohima was a vivid bustle. The main
street was swarming with pedestrians: a kinetic mosaic of
young men in flared trousers, older men in conservative suits,

girls in wrap-around bakhu-like skirts and some in mini-dresses or slacks, a very few men (mainly peasants bringing produce to market) in the traditional tribal wear of short and tight black kilt, open vest, feathers, beads and bamboo bracelets on calves and arms. But almost everyone sported bright shawls, chiefly of the Angami pattern. Our young guide for the morning, attired in a similar shawl, sniffed and said, 'Earlier, you could only wear them if you were a person of substance. Now everyone wears them. Earlier, men and women had strictly different styles, and the different tribes had different patterns, which they still do. But anyone wears anything now.' So much for democracy ...

The social scene in Kohima in the mornings literally revolves around the streets. People going to work or to college or shopping or just sauntering, meet and eddy a while in conversation, start walking away laterally, still talking, bump into another group, and the minuet goes on.

The entire street, though level, seems to be sliding and tilting in erratic progress, and if you want to get from point A to point B you generally find your way through a gregarious P, Q and R and maybe even an impulsive Z. We found this happening to us and fled for sanctuary in the nearby Kohima Cemetery.

In the green silence, the hysteria of guns was shrouded in the quiet of the neat rows of graves, over 1200 of them, each with its bronze litany of serial number, name, age, regiment and a fragment of distant memory: 14406177 Pvt. R.F. Clements, Royal Norfolk Reg., 6 May 1944, Age 19, 'Death divides but memory clings'; M TN/199706 Sepoy Jan Bahadur, Royal Indian Army Service Corps, 19 January 1945. Age 17. The youngest was sixteen. But the Japanese were stopped and the Empire dented but safe. Further up the slope, the district commissioner's (DC) tennis court, from either side of which guns blazed, is still marked out, a corner taken up by a monument. Close by is the cherry tree whose foliage concealed a Japanese sniper—a visiting Japanese not too long ago took back with him a souvenir cutting. A 'Commonwealth

Fund for War Cemeteries' keeps the place a pleasant park, the green slashed with the red of poinsettia, and lovers wander through it, unselfconscious in the ageless rites of death and regeneration.

From the rise of the cemetery we got our first panoramic view of Kohima, straggling along the hills spotted with the dazzle of wild sunflowers. Glinting tin roofs paraded along ridges and stumbled down slopes, streets growled with supply trucks—all of it with the self-inflated air which capitals everywhere have. The surrounding hillsides descended in the graceful contours of paddy-field terraces. Of the sixteen major tribes in Nagaland, only the Angamis, who live in Kohima district, practise terracing. The others pursue the nomadic 'jhum' cultivation which entails hacking down prime forest, drying and burning the vegetation, sowing the seeds and subsequently starting the whole cycle elsewhere. Since jhum is wasteful of forests (amongst Nagaland's prime resources) the government has been trying to discourage it but without marked success. In most of the areas we toured, sere brown scabs scarred the hills.

From the hush of the cemetery we ascended to the shrillness of the Little Flower School run by the Silesian nuns. The poetically named school, with its crowded classrooms and English-medium instruction (English is the official state language), is typical of the numerous missionary-run private schools in Nagaland. Besides these, there are also government schools where education is free. There are schools, at least primary schools, everywhere. Even in the remote villages, the nearest school house is generally no more than the width of a valley away. Nagaland has a lot of catching up to do; the literacy rate is under thirty per cent.

There are only four colleges in Nagaland, all in Kohima, with a total of 1300 students, and there are no postgraduate courses as yet. We visited the government-run Science College and the private Kohima Arts College. There is a generous system of scholarships, Rs 125 a month to any college student with a first-class school-leaving certificate, Rs 60 for a second class, and Rs 40 for a third. The colleges are co-educational and, like the schools, jam-packed with classes averaging over 150 pupils.

The most popular arts subjects appeared to be political science and economics for boys and education for girls. Student-teacher relationships seemed easy and relaxed, as did the intermingling between students of opposite sexes. 'We have a far less inhibited society than yours,' an arts student told me smugly. But when I asked him if dating was a popular campus pastime, he looked a bit crestfallen. 'Not really,' he replied. 'The girls can come out with us all right. But where are we to take them?' Kohima has one picture hall which shows old Hindi films and Italian spy thrillers on Sundays and a single music spot, Blue Haven, where every Saturday the Rivals perform 'sincere and sentimental numbers'.

The Nagas have an almost uncanny gift of music as their deep, perfectly counterpointed and harmonized tribal chants testify, and I was entertained to a choir of questions about the international and national pop world. Are the Beatles really going to get together again? Which is the best group in India today? What is the latest Grand Funk release?

A few of the more politically motivated students sneered on the sidelines, but I noticed that they tended to lean forward just a bit at the answers anyway. Politics is an integral part of campus life, as anywhere else, and likely to become more so with the Naga Student Federation getting more vocal. But for the present the average student attitude to politics is perhaps best summed up by what Angu Phizo, A.Z. Phizo's daughter, who is teaching education at the Kohima Arts College, said. Asked about her father and her own political beliefs, she replied, 'I haven't seen my father since '56. Of course I agree with some of his views. But active politics? No, I'm too involved in education to have much time for that.'

With the afternoon drawing to a close, we had a gargantuan Naga meal (steaming mounds of rice, a peppery pork stew, and boiled mustard leaves) at an eatery en route and headed for Kohima village. On the way to the village, through the bustle of the bazaar, we encountered our first and last Naga 'hostile'. Teki, on the constant lookout for picturesque tribal costumes to photograph and finding hardly any of these at all in the urban melting pot of Kohima, had developed an acute itch in his shutter finger. Driving through the market area we suddenly spotted, through the usual frieze of shawls and jackets, a burly figure in traditional garb—kilt, vest, armlets, feather and all. Teki shouted to our driver to stop, hopped off, and approached his barrel-chested subject who was buying paan at a roadside stall. Teki indicated he would like to take a photograph and the man muttered something, obviously a guttural refusal, shook his head, and turned back to the stall. Teki raised his camera and clicked. At the sound, his reluctant subject whirled around and, with booming voice and rolling gait, advanced upon Teki. From his walk and slurred voice it was evident that he had had a fairly liquid lunch. Teki fled for the car and we roared off, leaving the field to the irate but triumphant Naga and an amused circle of onlookers. 'Maybe you should have asked him to say "cheese" first,' I said in consolation.

Kohima village, 'the second largest village in Asia', is the old, dilapidated kernel from which the bureaucratic growth of Kohima town has sprouted. Each of the district towns, Mokokchung, Tuensang, Mon, has its parent village—poor but proud and self-contained relatives of the gleaming, tin-tacky towns they have willy-nilly spawned. These villages, the repositories of some of the old ways and customs, are governed by village headmen or elders according to tribal codes. Like accommodating parents, they are prepared to be influenced, but not dominated, by their urban progeny and live with them in amicable coexistence.

The road we were on became a steep kutcha track and bypassed a large, battered and carved wooden gate, propped up by wayside poles where the exigencies of changing times had flung it. The carvings on the gate were typical: elongated and primitively stylized male human figures suspended between the scimitar horns of buffalo heads. Someone in the car tried to explain the almost ineffable bond which the tribal Naga had with the buffalo, the beast's head being a symbol of identity for the man and expressing his prowess as hunter and domestic provider. There are four such disused gates in Kohima village, one for each of the four exogamous khels or clans. The khels are sub-units of each village and intra-khel marriage is proscribed by tribal law to prevent inbreeding.

As we climbed higher, the track became a rutted path, snuffling with pigs and jostled by shacks and small houses. The thatch roofs have mostly been replaced by rusty tin and corrugated iron though the bamboo weave walls still remain. The buffalo heads which used to hang above the doors to denote status have gone, but a few ersatz painted wooden ones can still be seen. The scarcity of shops is indicative of the economic symbiosis and yet separateness between village and town; the villagers take their produce down and do their shopping in the urban centre.

Trailed by the round-eyed curiosity of little children, we meandered up the village, through shadowy doorways, occasionally catching a rainbow glimpse of a woman weaving a shawl. The houses were crowded together and one of our guides remarked that the families, almost all agrarian, had their fields as much as two or three miles distant and their huddling together was a relic of the old warlike days of raids and head hunts when safety lay in numbers. Village granaries are built removed from the rest of the huts so that in case of a fire in the village the grain remains safe.

In a small courtyard we came across a late luncher, in tribal wear, eating out of a khupie, a three-legged dish-cum-stand carved out of a single block of wood. Teki clicked furiously and the man amiably proffered a spoon laden with pork and rice and chuckled at Teki's energetic refusal.

On our way out of the village we noticed a series of large stones, almost boulder-sized, about twenty of them spaced at regular intervals along the path. No one seemed to quite know what they were so we stopped an old man and asked him. His wrinkled face creased into a complicated smile.

Those, he informed us, old eyes sparkling and thin voice joshing the ingenuity and ignorance of youth, were memory stones. Men of means used to give great celebratory feasts in the old days, and then they would place a stone here to commemorate the occasion. Each stone was named and remembered after the man who had put it there. Why, he himself had given a feast many years ago, and put down a stone. His old open mouth quirked with silent laughter—at us, at the silent stones, and at his own once-young follies.

From Kohima we took a day trip to a village called Khonoma, twenty kilometres away. The road twisted and twined like a drunken snake, occasionally surprising everybody including itself by going straight for fifty feet. Khonoma has a typical Naga history of battle and pride and its fort was once famous for its strength and impregnability. Khonoma has also always been politically conscious. Phizo comes from here and so does Rano Shaiza, the president of the United Democratic Front (UDF). I was told that during the combing operations conducted by the army in 1956 and 1957, the entire population of the village deserted their homes and lived for weeks and months at a stretch in the forests, out of fear of a possible reprisal and a reluctance to help the forces of authority. Accompanying us on the trip was K. Silie, the twenty-one-year-old assistant editor of *Ura Mail*, the Kohima-based English-medium weekly sponsored by the UDF. Silie's family hails from Khonoma, from the same khel as Phizo, and Silie's parents still live there though he himself prefers an urban lifestyle and reflects his preference in an articulate awareness of the outside world and in his choice of modish clothes. Silie, with his Beatle-cropped hair and belled trousers and his easy familiarity with traditional customs, personifies contemporary Naga youth, poised between the old and the new, but with grace, not awkwardness.

We rounded a bend and saw Khonoma in the distance; a random cast of huts on a hump-backed ridge blanketed by a jungle, dominated by the ochre stone-and-stave walls of the old fort, now a military post. We drove up, parked and got out. Rough, stony footpaths knit the houses together, a few mud huts with thatch roofs, one or two concrete structures, and the rest made of bamboo weave and tin. The hill slopes and valleys beyond the village were mazy with bare terracing—the crops had been brought in and this was the time of the ten-day Terhungi post-harvest festival. There was an easy air of holiday. A ring of men in a courtyard sat drinking zu (rice beer) out of enormous wooden tankards, women gossiped and served more beer, children played and peeked at us. A hail of cordiality welcomed us as Silie explained who and what we were. We had come on the right day, we were told. Plenty of zu, said someone raising his tankard, and plenty of sport later when the wrestling would begin.

Explaining that his parents were not in the village that day, Silie asked us to accompany him to his cousin's home. The path took us up by a small tin-roofed house. 'Phizo's family home,' Silie casually indicated as we passed. We got to Silie's cousin's, a thatch hut with a packed earth courtyard fronting it on which millet-covered wicker mats, chickens, pigs and children basked in the wintry sun.

Silie's cousin, twenty-two-year-old Vitemelie, is one of the few non-Christians in the village. He and his father were drinking beer, seated on wooden stools under the low angle of the front roof, in the space where the farm tools are kept and visitors entertained. In the flurry of greetings, both the differences and the fundamental camaraderie between the two young men, almost of an age, were dramatically expressed. Silie in his tweed jacket and brown suede shoes and his cousin in Naga kilt and skull-cap tonsure with a thick topknot, one Christian and the other pagan animist, warmly embracing and clapping each other on their backs. We were seated and mugs of milky, frothy zu appeared. 'According to real custom,' said Silie, 'he should offer you sips from his own drink. But these things have changed. Actually, we Christians are not supposed to drink at all.' He took a vast swallow and added quite unnecessarily, 'But we do.' We all drank the zu, mild flavoured and slightly grainy with the stray particle of pounded rice. 'This is really very good stuff,' said Silie, 'very healthy and full of nutritional value.' We drank to our healthy values. The mistress of the household appeared with a metal canister and the mugs were refilled till zu slopped over the tops.

Through Silie we carried on a three-way conversation. I asked our young host if many people from the village had been out of Nagaland, visited other parts of the country. But I was politely referred to the father for answers—such things should be answered by elders. The old man harrumphed a bit and began telling us about his travels to Assam, mainly to get salt. Nagaland has no salt of its own and in the old days 'salt expeditions' to the neighbouring regions had to be periodically organized. While we talked, more and more zu was brought on and our mugs were kept brimful in keeping with relentless Naga hospitality. Sloshed with zu, I tried to cover my tankard with my hand but our host gently but firmly drew my wrist away while his sister poured me more home-brewed beer with smiling graciousness. Vitemelie grinned and indicated I drink up.

'He used to be very handsome and popular with girls till he had his accident,' said Silie. I looked at the lithely muscled, pleasant-faced young villager. His left profile was faintly scarred. 'What happened?' I asked. 'Oh, he came across a bear in the forest. Now he is very shy of his face, especially with girls.' There was a brief silence. 'Anyway,' said Silie, 'he finished the bear.' We all quaffed simultaneously.

Finally, awash with zu, we went down to the first terraced plot to watch the wrestling. A festive crowd of over a hundred people had already ringed the stubbly field, most of the men carrying canisters of beer. Every now and then some grizzled veteran, mountainous in the folds of his shawl, would rear up, holding high a grandson's or grand-nephew's arm, and rumble forth a challenge on behalf of the child. There would be general shouts of encouragement and good-natured raillery and then some other behemoth would erupt to his feet, holding up his young protégé's arm, and the challenge would be met. Laughing thunderously and looking like John Wayne playing a double role in *True Grit*, the old warriors would lead their charges to the centre of the arena, leave them there, and return to their positions. With whoops of delight, the diminutive combatants would peel off most or all of their clothes and set to, legs astraddle, arms locked behind each other's backs. Sway, tug, thrust, trip and a fall! Two falls and the winner was uproariously declared. As the tempo increased, there were at times half a dozen embattled teams on the field. Silie said, 'Nagas love wrestling. If there is a quarrel between two people they will settle it with a wrestling bout. You can still sometimes see it even in the towns.' I had a sharp mental flash of what might have happened if Teki hadn't been so quick hopping into the car in Kohima bazaar when he clicked his controversial camera the day before.

Squatting on the damp ground, watching the wrestling and the hills bright with wild sunflowers beyond, listening to the laughter and shouts over the water music of the two streams bifurcated by the ridge, I felt closer to the rhythm of Nagaland than I had during all the talk and political analyses that we had been into before. But, probably, it was just the zu.

From Khonoma we doubled back to Kohima and from there carried on to Tuensang, via the township of Wokha where we stopped for the night. The most memorable thing that happened to us at Wokha, home of the Lotha Nagas, was that we tried elephant's trunk. A rogue had been shot in the area a few days ago and the trunk, a delicacy, presented to the local DC, with whom we had dinner. The trunk, sliced and fried crisp, had a bitter, peculiarly fishy flavour and our host informed us that it was a potent aphrodisiac. Our night at Wokha however passed, as they say, without incident. Possibly the cold acts as an antidote.

Our jeep jounced and lurched through the six-hour journey to Tuensang to the tape-recorded beat of *Candida*. Tuensang, capital of Tuensang district, is a freshly minted town, shiny, but still a little rough at the edges. It has a population of 12,000 with the Government High School boasting a roster of 600 students, but the only two eateries in town shut down by 7 p.m. and the few shops much earlier. At the local council house-cum-tribal court, designed in the traditional morung or youth-dormitory style with a steep roof and with buffalo and lizard carvings on the supports, government officials in red shawls, who act as judges, can generally be seen busy at carroms. There is no public picture hall, no place really where young people, or old for that matter, can go. For our own part we went to Tuensang village, a brief drive away.

The village is a fairly large one, consisting of four khels connected by a broad unpaved 'main street'. We left our jeep outside and walked through, flanked by the quiet noontide shade of the huts. The men were all in the fields and the village was empty except for a few old women winnowing, children playing in the dust, and the ever-present, evil-eyed pigs in constant, snuffling search of food. The huts on either side with thick thatched roofs, higher in the front than the back, seemed like a silent swoop of short-necked, broad-winged birds in immobilized flight. Tuensang architecture is markedly different from that of Kohima, and has a strong similarity to the Dyak style of hut building, another point in favour of those who contend that the Nagas belong to an ethnic stock other than the Indo-Mongoloid or Kiratin group.

Modernity has come to the village like an unfinished jigsaw. As you stumble on a stone in the crude path, you glance down and see the half-hidden gleam of zinc piping which leads to a public brass faucet, one for each khel, and this one still coughing and spluttering water after a careless user. Or some movement above you catches your eye and you look up at a plaited dried-grass roof ornament and for the first time notice the silent tautness of electricity wires running overhead.

The huts, however, still retain a traditional uniform pattern. A twenty-five-to-thirty-foot long, sloping central ridgepole runs the length of the hut and the sides of the roof angle down sharply from it. The front of the hut consists of a ground-level open porch where work-a-day implements are stored and domestic chores performed. Status-establishing mithun and buffalo heads adorn the supporting pillars, and stringed skulls of squirrels, monkeys, and birds hang in musty festoons. 'Earlier, you could see a lot of human heads as well,' said our guide. 'Now they have all been thrown away.'

The Nagas practised head-hunting in the old days. Every now and again a village, for reasons of revenge or just pure hell-raising, would raid a neighbouring village and claim their victims' heads as trophies of war, bring them triumphantly back to their own village, boil them and peel off the flesh and scalp, and then display the skulls as emblems of prowess and courage. Though there have been no officially reported and verified incidents of head-hunting in Nagaland for almost twenty years, the Nagas are still very sensitive about this aspect of their past. A village Christian will, with vehement ignorance, try to brush the whole matter under the carpet of no-comment. An urban sophisticate if asked about head-hunting will probably respond with angry pride and scorn at your ignorance of the progress achieved in Nagaland. But now and then, in unwary conversation, a chance remark dropped or an intonation stressed might indicate to you that the speaker feels that possibly the bad old days weren't quite as unmitigatedly reprehensible as all that.

Walking through the village we came across another customary feature cast up and stranded by the receding tide of old traditions. It was one of the big pirogue-like war drums of Tuensang, abandoned by the path and clucking with pecking hens. Though a few of the drums still occupy their positions in the open-sided protective huts specially designed for them, they are seldom sounded any longer. The club-like drumsticks are mostly missing and the drums themselves are often used as litter bins. Some anthropologists claim that the drums reflect an ancient legacy, and are really upturned ocean-going canoes and that the forgotten ancestors of the Nagas were voyagers from Polynesia. We traced our way back, noticing the frequent yellow tin signs along the way which quoted chance sentences, sometimes just phrases, from the Bible in black characters of schoolboy care.

A few minutes later we were back in the neat raw town, sitting in a government official's living room, lined and decorated with miniature tribal spear souvenirs, talking to his son who had just completed his exams and was wondering which college and course to join and when, while the Beatles in a corner whispered words of wisdom on stereo, *Let it be*.

From Tuensang we dog-legged to Mon via Mokokchung where we put up for the night. Mokokchung, population 17,000 in 1972, is in the Ao tribe zone. It is the district capital and an important commercial centre and a smaller, somewhat less earnest version of Kohima. The young people who gather most evenings at the Holiday Inn—a large student-run restaurant, where Mokokchung's best beat group, the Contenders, often plays—seem more into pop than politics. There is somehow a freer, easier air about Mokokchung in comparison to which Kohima, in retrospect, appears just a little stilted. The Aos have a tradition of social fluidity and their system of elected village panchayats is one of the most notably democratic features of Naga tribal life.

A bone-jarring, grimy journey from Mokokchung brought us to Mon, the newest and most backward of Nagaland's four districts. Mon is the home of the Konyaks, the original naked Nagas, the largest and most primitive of all the tribes. The road had long petered out to a jeep track and night had fallen before we caught the far firefly winking of the lights of Mon town. The distant lights, getting closer, slipped in and out of the darkness as we took the unending bends in the track, and then all of a sudden we were there and the Circuit House had beds for us but no food. Some arcane god for weary travellers must have interceded on our behalf because we managed to find a ramshackle dhaba and wake its owner, an ancient Sylhetese whom we finally cajoled into serving us tear-streaming hot curry and parathas cold as an Eskimo's epitaph.

The next morning we had our first clear look at Mon, a smaller model of Tuensang, toy-bright bungalows dotting hill slopes lower and gentler than in most other parts of the state, thickly forested ridges swelling to the horizon at which the DC pointed and said, 'Beyond that lies Burma.' We wandered through the town, mainly offices and officials' residences, a few shops, mostly motor parts and general goods, and, quite inexplicably, a photograph studio.

We took a steep, rough gradient out of town to visit the village of Chui and meet its famous Angh or king. The Angh of Chui is the biggest of the hereditary Anghs of Nagaland and has some twenty-two villages or about 15,000 to 20,000 people under his now nominal suzerainty. The Anghs were absolute rulers, with powers of life and death over their subjects, till British policy began to erode their autocracy from mid-1930 onwards. Since Independence the Anghs have been vested with a residue of traditional and voluntary respect and nothing more.

As our jeep ground its way up the track, we passed small bands of Konyaks carrying bundles of firewood and long-handled machete-like daos. The patchwork of encroaching civilization has caused these once naked Nagas to adopt a few scraps of clothing, loin cloths, and even an occasional shirt. Many of the women however are still bare-breasted and most of the men wear the excruciatingly tight broad metal waistbands from which depends the front half of a loin cloth.

We went past several jungle-fringed hamlets and finally got to Chui, a village of 200 huts and about 1000 people divided into four khels. The thatch-and-bamboo Konyak huts are different again from those of Tuensang, the rounded curve of the front section of the roofs making them vaguely reminiscent of giant Alpine hats. As our jeep stopped, a cacophony of children ringed us, and our dubhashiya or interpreter led us to the Wanghem, the Angh's 'palace'. The 'palace' is an outsize hut, 150 feet long and about 30 feet high from the ground to its ridge pole, built on the same design as the other huts but about four times larger. The Angh needs the extra elbow room as he has a wife (Wangchu), fifteen concubines and forty children. The Wanghem, rebuilt on its original site about six years ago, took 400 voluntary workers a month to construct. The command of such free labour is one of the privileges still extended to the Angh by his people.

The entire front of the palace, with its four carved-wood roof supports, is studded with old skulls—mithun, buffalo, elephant, monkey, and human. There are still about 200 left of the latter, racked up against the front wall and held in position by bamboo spikes driven through the jawbone cavities. We trooped into the murky interior—high, smoke-blackened and strung with mangy, crudely stuffed trophies of the hunt. In the dim recesses of the deep front room, across the uneven packed earth floor, we saw the Angh seated before a small open fire, the gloom shot with the bronze of the flames and the shifting highlights on his high-cheekboned, green-tattooed face, framed by the seven-inch curve of mountain goat horns (chingom) piercing the lobes of his ears.

Our interpreter performed the introductions and said the Angh had succeeded his father at the age of twenty and had been ruling for thirty-six years. I blinked and asked him to repeat this for in the half dark the Angh looked no more than in his mid-thirties. But he is in fact a well-knit, unlined fifty-six. I asked if, in the old days, he had taken any heads. The tone of the reply was stiff with a disused pride. Yes, he said, the last one thirty-two years ago, bringing his tally to six. I noticed though that the amulet around his neck only had four brass heads. With my eyes getting used to the dark, I noted three yellowed calendar prints, of Gandhi, Rajendra Prasad and a youthful Nehru, 'In Pensive Mood'. I asked if the Angh had ever been outside Nagaland. No, he replied, his home was here. But he was a friend of India and bore goodwill towards it. We asked him if he would step into the

light for a few photographs. He agreed readily and then added
with a touch of peevishness that we must send him copies.
Lots of people came and took his pictures and said they would
send him some and no one ever did. We promised to send
him copies and he busied himself elaborately tying his
topknot.

The sunlight seemed somehow to shrink him as he posed
self-consciously for the camera, his chingom, face tattoo,
traditionally blackened teeth, and topknot at diminished
variance with a cheap bazaar pullover and a pair of sere blue
shorts. As he squatted on the low broad rock slab outside his
house where in the old days the freshly taken heads would
be proudly displayed, the chant of a hymn arose from a small
hut facing the Wanghem. 'That's the Church,' said our guide.
'Most of the people in the village are now Christians. The
Angh has insisted on it. But he himself and his family remain
non-Christian.'

Zephyrs of change are breathing over Chui, the aspirations
of the young decrying old customs such as face tattooing,
teeth blackening and the keeping of concubines. Even the
morung, the tribal youth dormitory which commonly houses
males from the age of twelve to marriage, has a dilapidated
air and the torch reeds in the rafters, stored there in case of
midnight emergency, look damp and unusable. The Angh in
his own person reflects the approaching end of traditional
continuity, for though he has many sons, his wife, the
Wangchu, has yet to bear him a son and acceptable heir.
Failing this, the Angh-ship will pass on to the present Angh's
younger brother, who lives in the village and does have a
legal heir.

On our way out of the village, we went by the chapel,
now empty. With its bamboo-bench pews, and a dais with a
desk and a blackboard behind it, it looked like a village
classroom. As we walked to the jeep, an old man, near naked,
with an incredibly convoluted face and a small child slung
papoose fashion across his back, approached us. He grinned
gapingly, we grinned back, and Teki clicked. The village

children, now that our impending departure had made us strangers again, had gathered around once more, laughing and chattering about us, about the old man. Our guide offered him a cigarette and he happily accepted, waving the smoke and the excitement of the children away.

The downward giddy track with its twists and turns seemed to spin these and other impressions of our tour round in my mind and I wondered how and what I would write. I remembered what an earnest young student leader had said to me in Kohima: 'Whatever you do, write the truth about Nagaland.' A friend of his had interjected: 'And the truth is that people treat it as a problem in politics when it is really just a question of people, who have been turned into a problem.'

The problem has the contours of a vicious circle. As a young Naga put it, 'You people say you want us to be like you, yet when you came here you had to get special permission and if I want a passport I have to apply all the way to Delhi.' Under the Bengal Eastern Frontier Regulation of 1873, non-Naga visitors require Inner Line Permits. The 'inner line' policy was originally formulated to ensure that the eastern hill people did not get swamped by an unrestricted influx from the more progressive plains, and today it is fairly simple for an Indian citizen to get a permit, which costs fifty paise. Despite its easy availability, the permit still casts a psychological shadow of a dividing paper curtain. The Central view is that relaxations can only be made after it is considered safe to do so and the situation has been 'normalized'. The majority of Naga opinion, however, holds that the 'situation' will continue till the tensions arising from restraints are relaxed. In both cases the vocabularies of argument are direct and basic—only the languages seem to differ.

So what's the solution, the answer to the Naga question?

The 'answer' was given by twenty-four-year-old Allem Longkumer, former vice-president of the Naga Student Federation and secretary of the Student Action Committee for Peace, who is currently and desultorily reading for an

MA degree in literature from Dibrugarh University. Allem spoke with soft but firm conviction: 'I'll tell you what we really believe in. We believe in peace. We are children of rebellion. All our lives we have seen trouble and unrest. We are sick of it. Whatever is the political future of Nagaland, we want peace.'

He took out his diary which contains three pictures—of Joan Baez, of Billy Graham (who in November 1972 preached to a vast gathering on the Kohima football ground) and of Fidel Castro. 'My three heroes,' he smiled and extracted a sheet of paper from the diary. 'It's a song which a friend of mine wrote and sang at a student meeting.' I unfolded the sheet and read:

> I will meet you in the morning
> When there'll be peace in our land.
> Then be very faithful dear friends,
> For you'll not have long to wait.
> There'll be peace for us in the
> Morning over there.
> If you hasten out to glory, linger
> Near the Eastern Gate. For
> A new dawn will be breaking.
> So you'll not have long to wait.
> Keep your spirit high and burning.
> For the big day watch and wait,
> That day will be like heaven,
> When there'll be peace in our land.
> There'll be peace for us in the
> Morning over there.

Jilling Out with Steve

The ultimate getaway? No two ways about it: It's Jilling.
Who, what, where is Jilling. Shhh ... Listen to the silence.
That's Jilling.

Ex-fighter pilot and former tea planter, fifty-eight-year-old Steve Lall is today a retailer of the country's most priceless and endangered commodity. Together with his wife Parvati, he zealously guards his product for an exclusive clientele who come to sample it at Jilling: forty-five acres of densely wooded Kumaon hillside, 6500 feet above sea level, 300 kilometres from Delhi and thirty-eight kilometres from the rail head at Kathgodam.

Cloaked in a lush, multicultural forest of oak and chestnut and deodar, with brief but bewitching views of Nanda Devi, Jilling is part of the erstwhile Stiffles estate and was bought in 1965 by Steve's mother who is said to have got it for the price of a second-hand car. Taken together with the contiguous tracts owned by neighbours, Jilling runs to some 140 acres of a customized Eden, a perfect place for chilling out. Scattered over the hillside at discreet intervals are four wood-and-stone cottages, simply but comfortably furnished, for visitors. Natural trails ramble through the woods, inviting exploration: from the seven-kilometre-long, level Lovers' Walk, to steeper hikes that lead up to the ridge from where the valley on the farther side falls away in an escarpment as sudden and swift as the swoop of a falcon.

There is good, wholesome home cooking, eclectically crammed bookshelves to browse through, and, in the evening, blazing bonfires spiralling sparks into star-filled skies. There are no telephones, no TV, no cars. This is the secret of Steve's unique product, which is silence.

In a world where frenetic movement is mistaken for progress, strident rhetoric for the inflexion of discourse, it is Jilling's silence that sets it apart. When Bunny and I spent three days there, I sat on the sunlit lawn outside our cottage and listened to the silence.

The first thing that strikes you about silence is that it is not an absence of sound, for that would make it a sterile vacuum. Listening to silence is like watching a glass being filled with water, drop by careful drop. When the glass is full, the water brims over the top without spilling, the convex curve of liquid held in place like a drawn bowstring. The silence I listened to at Jilling was like that resonant arc, a supple filament that strung together the ratcheting feathers of a partridge in flight, the sharp call of a barking deer, the leafy conversation of trees, the bubbles of air exploding in the bottle of soda on the table.

I realized that the silence was a gift as fragile as the finest porcelain, as evanescent as the shimmer of a butterfly's wings. Like most gifts worth the getting, or the giving, Jilling's silence is hard won; it is based on uncompromising solitude. The nearest motorable road is two kilometres away, where guests can park their cars. From there it is a brisk forty-minute climb to Jilling; for those faint of limb or heart, ponies or palkies are provided.

Jilling's deliberate isolation has kept at bay what Steve calls the 'tootak tootak tootian' Marutized holidaymakers from the plains. If anyone tries to build a road up here, I'll shoot the bugger, says Steve in what is surely a joke—I think. He is similarly adamant about forest conservation. He is convinced that afforestation programmes, based on quick-growing species like pine, have resulted in monocultural man-made forests which eventually deplete the soil and lead to the catastrophe of topsoil erosion and the environmental degradation sweeping our hills. Steve believes in a policy of non-intervention, of allowing the natural medley of the forest to rejuvenate itself through the unforced diastole and systole of its own great green beating heart.

But, despite its solitude and Steve's ecological evangelism, there is nothing sombre or sanctimonious about Jilling's bracing air, infused with the rich earthiness of the village community living on its periphery and in perfect harmony with it. Tara Devi, a sprightly widow and mother of ten, drops in while we are there. She reports a rogue bear which has mauled two women cutting grass, and almost in the same breath mentions a daughter-in-law who is getting fat, an ominous sign of indulgence. She herself is well, except that try as she might she cannot achieve a bowel movement more than once a week. I suggest that she drink a bottle of beer daily to ease her malady. The thought of drinking Angrezi sharab at sixty-five rupees a bottle makes Tara Devi cackle so hard that she swears that the demon gripping her innards has been exorcized straightaway.

A baby barking deer—huge liquid eyes, velvet button of a nose and twitching ears, Bambi incarnate—is found by a grass cutter and brought to Jilling. The mother has probably been taken by a leopard, of which there are at least three in the area. A spirited debate ensues, the fate of the fawn in the balance. No-nonsense Steve is all for putting it back in the forest, letting nature take its course. Parvati and his daughter, Nandini, are equally vehement about harbouring the waif till it can find its adult feet in the wild. Fortunately, as is usual in the hills, the womenfolk have their way. Steve grumbles but looks pleased as Punch.

When it is time to leave, Bunny and I are not in the least sad. Quite the contrary. For we know, deeper than any words, that having once experienced Jilling and its silence we can never really leave it, but will return again and again. Our goodbye is also a greeting.

That's all very well, but how the hell does one actually get there? Well, that's just it you see. Jilling, as I said, is a gift. And as a gift, you can't just go there and claim it; you have to wait till it is given to you, when you have earned it. And once you have, let others also earn it for themselves. Remember: to ensure Jilling's code of silence which makes it incomparable, mum's the word.

Tal Tales from the Hills

This is an anthropological expedition. It focuses on two distinct and inimical species: the LIT and the GIHM. Thanks to the Darwinian process of the survival of the fittest, the LIT has become almost extinct. Its territory has largely been appropriated by the ever-increasing hordes of GIHM.

Read on to find out which species you belong to. Or want to belong: LIT or GIHM? The latter being, literally, a never-say-die lot ...

All of a sudden at Haldwani the hills are around you, bounding up like big, friendly, shaggy dogs proffering welcoming licks with tongues of cool mist. Past the traffic snarls of Haldwani, you are in Kathgodam and the road begins to climb into the green hills and valleys of the Tal country, the lake district of Kumaon comprising Nainital and the lesser-known Bhimtal, Sattal and Naukuchiyatal. Like Mussoorie, Nainital has long ago been turned into an overbuilt concrete junk heap stuck on a hill. But Bhimtal and the other lakes hold out a promise of a relatively unspoilt tranquillity.

It was an appealing promise for the six of us, keen on getting away for the long Independence Day weekend from the din of the 'Freedom at Fifty' celebrations in Delhi. We were booked at the Country Inn resort, billed as a haven of uncluttered peace and quiet. Situated on a gentle slope 4500 feet above sea level, with a distant view of the lake set like a blue-green unblinking eye in the socket of the valley, it would truly be such a haven—were it not for the GIHM: the Great Indian Holiday Maker.

Fifty years after Independence, ours is a deeply divided society, chasmed with fissures of caste, class, and creed. The contours of most such rifts have been mapped, charted, and deplored with proper political correctness. A notable exception is the gulf separating the GIHM from his minority counterpart, the LIT, or Lesser Indian Traveller. It is a significant divide, based on the axiom that it is not just what a country does when it is doing something that tends to separate it but also what it does when it is not doing anything and is on vacation.

On vacation, LITs like to go to places where there is hardly anybody, including other LITs. GIHMs like to go to places where there is everybody, preferably other GIHMs. The GIHM is motivated by a great fear: the fear of becoming bore. As in: *Yaar, hum toh barre bore ho gaye.* Becoming bore is a condition which the GIHM dreads more than death itself, and he has devised any number of stratagems to keep at bay this fate worse than dissolution. GIHM prescriptions to stave off becoming bore include video parlours, boating on lake, horse riding on Mall, papri chaat shops redolent of recycled hajmi masala, transistorized Indi-pop played at full blast, two-tone Maruti horns sounded every minute on the minute, and, most importantly, the presence of other GIHMs.

For the GIHM, solitude is worse than solitary confinement; it is the ultimate quandary of solipsism: If I am the only one around how do I know that I'm around at all, or if it's just around that's around? This is much worse than becoming bore; it's the very essence of boreness.

The great enemy of the GIHM is silence and to combat it he generates as much noise as he can to advertise his presence to other GIHMs who rally round and add to the decibel level. Since constant exposure to amplified din has rendered most GIHMs hard of hearing, the considerate GIHM also leaves behind a visual trail of plastic bags, empty soft-drink bottles, Frooti packs, and silver foil gutka wrappers as an aid to congregation.

When we got there, Bhimtal was awash with GIHMs. Taking evasive action we retreated to nearby Garuntal, a small, little-known spot where there is literally nothing. Except for a lake as still and shiny as a sheet of glass, serried ranks of pines standing silent sentinel on the surrounding hillsides, and a soft breeze quickened with birdsong.

Woh kya kar rahe hain, Papaji? squeaked the voice of an infant GIHM. Spotting our vehicle parked by the road, a family of GIHMs had pulled up to see what unpublicized tamasha was in the offing in this unlikely place. We stared at the lake; the GIHMs stared at us. Seeing two cars parked on the road, a third car stopped. What they are doing? asked the newcomers excitedly, not wanting to miss out on whatever action was going. Don't know, yaar, replied the first lot. They are only standing and looking at water, how they are not getting bore, we are not knowing. Another car pulled up. More spectators. By now we had two options. Either sell tickets to the show we were providing, or flee. We fled.

We discovered we had a fatal attraction for GIHMs. They seemed to follow wherever we went. We went to Sattal; droves of GIHMs. Naukuchiyatal; throngs of them. Bunny and I finally took off for Ranikhet, which I had last been to thirty-seven years ago with my uncle Hemrajbhai, who had told me that he had it on good authority, from a man who knew Dr B.C. Roy, that the then chief minister of Bengal highly recommended Ranikhet as a place so deserted that one could walk nude down the Mall without provoking comment. In the event, Hemrajbhai and I did not walk nude down the Mall. But the point was taken; Ranikhet was deserted.

Ranikhet Mall was deserted thirty-seven years later when Bunny and I walked down it. It was pouring cats and dogs and we were soaked to the skin. But no sooner had we ducked for refuge into the West View Hotel—where I had stayed thirty-seven years ago—than a booming voice barged in demanding of the harried manager the price of a family suit. Papa GIHM had arrived on the scene. *Suit nahin, suite bolte hain*! corrected Mama GIHM. Hearing the magical sound 'sweet', the Baba Log GIHMs set up a choric wail: *Sweety chahiye, sweety chahiye*!

Rain or no rain, Bunny and I fled again. Uttam, our driver, took us back to Bhimtal by an alternative route—a kachha jeep track that wriggled like an earthworm over the now sunlit hills, passing tiny stone-and-slate villages, several of whose residents hitched a ride on the jeep, smelling of woodsmoke and sun and hard work, confidingly informative about the price of cauliflowers and guavas, the local crops of the season.

It was one of the best drives Bunny and I have ever had, in the hills or anywhere else. I hope the hitch-hikers thought it a nice ride too.

Back in our elegantly appointed cottage at Country Inn, we congratulated ourselves for having at last broken the GIHM jinx. We might have spoken too soon. For, as the shadows deepened in the valley below and the wind soughed through the trees and the rolling mist nudged insistently at the window panes, we did what all people in all hills do. We told each other ghost stories. Brian told us about a ghost with a fez in Calcutta. Sameer recounted a daylight encounter with a lady ghost in Baroda. Ganimat narrated eerie goings-on in her family house in north Delhi. Suddenly, the cottage was full of unseen, jostling presences clamouring for attention. And a sudden thought struck me. What if old GIHMs never die but only seem to fade away to become spooks and come back to haunt us when we least expect them to? The ultimate revenge of those who would rather give up the ghost than become bore.

Penthouse Boat, Yes?

We last went to Kashmir in 1987—while it was still a tourist and not a terrorist destination. Not that there weren't hazards for the unwary visitor. Like double-decker houseboats. And double helpings of implacable cabbage.

To hear the 'famous travel-writer person' tell it, it was like Noah's Ark revisited. 'And there were rats, my dear, that big, and cockroaches, and ... '

As she was talking about a Srinagar houseboat, I didn't believe a word of it. A rat would be out of the race altogether, and a cockroach—the only species believed to be capable of surviving a nuclear holocaust—knows better than to lock horns with a Kashmiri houseboat owner, a breed apart when it comes to dealing with non-paying guests, human or otherwise.

Said to be the invention of an expatriate Englishman who devised it to get around the local law prohibiting non-Kashmiris from owning immovable property in the state, the houseboat has become a symbol of Srinagar, rather like the canals of Venice: redolent of a somewhat murky romanticism.

Srinagar houseboats range from the grimy hulks along the Jhelum to the festal armada of 'deluxe' craft moored on the Dal and Nagin lakes complete with striped awnings, chandeliers, wall-to-wall views of the surrounding hills and sun-decks suitable for striking vaguely nautical poses while keeping an eye open for the bikini off to starboard.

'And are there ... er ... ' I'm inevitably asked. The better class houseboats are indeed equipped with 'ers'—mainline water, flush potty, geysers, bathtubs and all—and exotic acrobatics along the hull are not necessary for the performance of ablutions. The perils and pitfalls of houseboat life are far more subtle.

All licensed houseboats have a category rating with which the tariffs, inclusive of meals, are fixed. Such fetters on the spirit of free enterprise, however, do not deter the houseboat owner from pursuing the policy that the customer is always ripe for the plucking.

The approved design of deluxe-class houseboats comprises three bedrooms, with attached baths, plus dining room and separate sitting room. Canny owners, however, have been known to put up a second, smaller storey on this structure, thus getting two houseboats for the price of one-and-a-half, at the expense of the guests' privacy.

'Double-deck houseboat!' brightly beamed the proprietor of one I was taken to. Seeing me look dubious he cajoled: 'Penthouse boat, yes?' his hands describing parabolas in the air, suggestive of the curvaceous delights popularly associated with that term.

'No penthouse,' I declared firmly. 'No basement either. No split-level. No duplex. Regular houseboat, one. Okay?' 'Okay,' he sniffed sulkily, and, looking like Charles Laughton being offloaded after the mutiny on the *Bounty*, accompanied me to the waiting shikara (a slim lake transportation craft) to find a 'regular houseboat, one' to my liking.

Houseboat menus are another testimony to local ingenuity as evidenced by changes it can bring to recipes based on the humble cabbage. 'No more cabbage,' I declared after two days of this. 'Wazwan now,' I insisted, referring to the traditional banquet consisting largely of mutton dishes. 'Wazwan last week,' was the mournful response, suggesting I had missed out on a cosmic treat. 'Wazwan,' I repeated. 'Tomorrow,' I added.

The morrow came and no wazwan. 'Where's wazwan?' I demanded, in the pidgin newspeak that is the lingua franca of tourist Kashmir. It turned out there was no wazwan to be had that day. It was too cold. The next day it was too hot. It seems that Kashmiri sheep are remarkably susceptible to the slightest climatic aberration, which immediately renders them unfit for translation into wazwan.

We waited all week for wazwan weather, but it never came. Only the cabbage did—steamed, boiled or curried, for lunch and for dinner—with an inexorability matched only by that of the water-borne salesmen who swept down on our houseboat in their gondola-like shikaras, proffering wares ranging from factory-fresh antiques to shawls spun from a yarn that owed more to the seller's eloquence than to the pashmina goat from which it was purportedly derived; from wooden bric-a-brac of ersatz walnut to topaz stones made from genuine cut glass.

'All very nice things, all very cheap,' intoned Abdul, the houseboat's major domo, with the bland assurance of a commission agent assured of his kickback. 'You see, you like, you buy. Not like, not buy. You see, okay?'

Since the only other entertainment on offer was playing scrabble with a set apparently consisting of only 'Zs' and 'Xs' or reading the houseboat's selection of paperbacks that inevitably had the last page missing so you never did discover who had slit Colonel Carruthers's throat in the library with a frozen poppadam of oriental design, we agreed to see, okay—but only see, mind.

It was a case of they came, we saw, they conquered. I drew the line finally at the imitation rabbit-fur-lined Hush Puppies and we beat a strategic retreat via the aft gangplank to the pier where a fortuitous shikara that called itself 'Leaping Lola Ha-Ha, Full Spring Seats' bore us away across the shimmering expanse of the lake, leaving in our wake, like dying ripples, the plaintive cries of 'Very nice, very cheap. You like, you buy'.

Shikaras, whether used as a means of escape or merely for an excursion, are part and parcel of a houseboat holiday. A Srinagar shikara ride is an unforgettable experience: drifting in the golden glow of twilight, the encircling hills veiled with gossamer mist as pearly pink as the petals of the lotus blooming on the lake, through the cool waters of which you trail your fingers, dreamily wondering if the tiny fish nibbling your cuticle is a potential carrier of AIDS.

'It's just like being in a gondola,' said my companion. 'Do you think the boatman might sing for us?' Our lugubrious paddler perked up at once. 'I sing, yes,' he affirmed and launched into a song. We couldn't follow the lyrics, but there weren't very many of these anyway. Most of the time was taken up by gusty sighs unexpectedly punctuated by tremolo ululations as the sun set and the moon came up and the stars shone down their benign radiance—all the better for the clouds of mosquitoes that had gathered to see and sting us by.

'Did you pay him something extra for singing?' my companion asked, when we were back on the houseboat. 'No,' I admitted, 'I paid him for shutting up.'

And we walked into the dining room to face the cabbage.

At Cross Purposes
in 'Little Tibet'

The first thing you notice when you get to Ladakh, which we did in 1990, is that it looks more like Tibet than Tibet does. The phrase 'lunar landscape' has become a stock prop for travel writers in describing Ladakh.

We got to Ladakh when political and social tensions between the local Buddhists and Muslims were rife. Willy-nilly, we found ourselves being made party to the schism: Don't take a Muslim taxi driver to a Buddhist monastery, or you won't be let in, we were warned.

Fortunately, on our last day there, we were instrumental in effecting a mini reconciliation. And to my credit, I didn't use 'lunar landscape' even once. I cheated. I used 'moonscape'.

We stop for the obligatory snapshot at Fotu La pass, at 13,479 feet above sea level, the highest point on the Srinagar-Leh highway that writhes like a black whiplash down the rock-ribbed mountainside. The cries of swooping magpies echo an eerie epiphany: Zanskar, the lost kingdom; Dras, the coldest human habitation in the world; the haunted Daliesque moonscape of Lamayuru, the oldest shrine in Ladakh. Tossing aside my mental thesaurus, I stare wordlessly at a laconic landscape that challenges description.

'CAMPING SITE—JULAY,' reads a sign. I smile at the misspelling of July. 'Julay,' corrects our driver-cum-guide. 'It means "namaste", have a good day.' The correction brings home the truism that the tourist is an interloper at cross purposes with the inherent theme of things.

Ladakh is a reverse image of Kashmir. Kashmir's verdant lushness is translated here into an awesome bleakness, a windswept emptiness where yaks graze like ambulatory ebon haystacks under sentinel outcrops crowned with the cubist lava of ancient gompas emergent from the living rock. The political landscape provides an equally stark contrast. Militant secessionism in Kashmir is mirrored in Buddhist-majority Leh by a demand to break with allegedly pro-Muslim Srinagar and be given Union Territory status under direct Central control.

The violence that erupted in Leh last summer entangled a social skein as intricate as the weave of a pashmina shawl, comprising the ethnic threads of the Mons, the Dards, the Baltis, and the Tibetans, brought together over the centuries when Leh was a pivotal point on the silk route between China and India.

Simmering discontent reached flashpoint in July 1989 when a minor scuffle escalated to an outburst that claimed four lives in police firing: three Buddhist demonstrators, and a Muslim village woman hit by a stray bullet. Though there has been no violence since then, several broken glass panes in Leh bazaar identify closed Muslim establishments while Buddhist shops now display their names in Tibetan as well as Roman script. Ladakh's current troubles are a spillover of the Kashmir problem. 'PAKISTANI AGENTS—GO BACK!' says a slogan scrawled on a village wall. But here, as elsewhere, tourism has had its own dubious part to play. In a wry aftermath to last year's incidents, in which several shops and hotels were stoned and forcibly shut down, refugees from neighbouring villages have sought sanctuary in the tourist bungalow in Leh.

The rich harvest of Ladakh's burgeoning tourism industry—which before last year's turmoil registered 15,000 foreign visitors annually—was perceived to be harvested mainly by the hoteliers and tour operators of Leh's Sunni community with its Srinagar connections. 'The majority of Muslims in Ladakh are Shias. But we've all been tarred with the same brush,' says a Muslim resident of Leh.

The continuing social and economic boycott of the Muslims by the Ladakh Buddhist Association has created a rift deeper than the gorge of the Senge Chhu, the local name for the Indus. The schism has split families with matrimonial links across the communal divide. 'My mother was Buddhist before she converted to Islam to marry my father when she was nineteen. But recently when she was sick, her Buddhist brother couldn't visit her for fear of the boycott,' says a senior spokesman for Leh's Muslim community. 'The Dalai Lama himself has repeatedly stressed that true Buddhism has tolerance for all religions. But the LBA has ignored his pleas. They've even invited BJP leaders up to Ladakh to make public speeches. I think Dr Ambedkar would have appreciated the irony of the situation.'

A Buddhist spokesman, acknowledged by moderates on both sides for his secular views, admits that the boycott movement has been taken over by 'misguided elements', mainly economically frustrated youths. But then adds, 'Do you know what the retort of my Muslim friends was to the boycott? They said, "You are boycotting us now? We've been socially boycotting you for years." At our festivals, they couldn't of course drink chhang. But the mullahs had even started enforcing the Islamic proscription of music, which has always been part of our common Ladakhi heritage.' Fundamentalism is a chasm with two walls.

'Make sure you take a car with a Buddhist driver when you visit the gompas,' we were told, 'or the lamas won't let you in.' In 'Little Tibet', religion has appropriated tourism. Or is it the other way round?

At Thiksey monastery, the dim interior is lambent with the glow of butter lamps, like a living carpet of fireflies. Then a helpful monk throws a switch and glaring neon dispels the magical effect. 'Dalai Lama,' he proudly points to a Polaroid snapshot on an altar. In Spituk gompa, an exquisitely sculpted Tara smiles enigmatically at a votive bowl full of cellophane-wrapped Parry's toffees, courtesy Indian Airlines, while an American visitor looks on bemusedly. On a wall, a chrome-plated clock partly obscures a timeless fading fresco. What do you do when you've 'done' Nirvana? Or had it done for you, in pre-packaged modernism designed to suit every taste and itinerary. It is fortunate that Buddhism is a forgiving religion, for in the trespasses prompted by tourism it has not a little to forgive.

The urgently felt need to preserve a balance between the cultural and economic pitfalls of tourism and the solipsism of a 'living museum' screened off from outside influences has given rise to organizations like the Ladakh Ecological Development Group (LEDG) and the Students' Educational and Cultural Movement of Ladakh (Secmol). Descended from the Ladakh Project, founded in 1978 by a Swedish linguist, Helena Norbeg-Hodge, LEDG is a non-governmental agency funded by Norwegian Agency for Development Co-operation (NORAD) and individual donors from all parts of the world who support its aim of 'development based on Ladakh's own resources and traditional values'. LEDG's activities include propagating the use of solar energy and appropriate irrigation systems and heightening awareness among both Ladakhis and visitors of the area's unique physical and cultural environment. The organization has produced the first book on ecology in the Ladakhi language, written and illustrated by a committee member.

Secmol, started in 1988 by an engineering graduate, Sonam Wanchuk, seeks to promote traditional art forms by organizing regular cultural shows in Leh with a view to ensuring that Ladakhi folkways remain economically and intrinsically viable. In such an effort, however, tourism has an ambivalent role to play, fostering both prosperity and a potential divisiveness whereby 'reciprocal relations of mutual aid break down'.

A commentator has cited the tradition of the need-based sharing of village resources. The owner of two pack horses, who customarily would lend one to a needy neighbour, is less likely to be accommodative if newly created market forces place an opportunity-cost on the loaning of the animal, which otherwise might be hired out for cash, thus engendering a spiral of economic and social inequality. And when it is not just a beast of burden that is in the balance but the perceived expropriation of a marketable culture in its entirety, the spiral can become a self-destructive maelstrom. Like fundamentalism, tourism also can have two walls.

On our last day in Ladakh, a local acquaintance tries to dispel these gloomy thoughts. Thanks to us, he says, he has managed to organize an evening of 'secular music'. Two noted singers, a Muslim and a Buddhist, have agreed to a joint performance in our guest house. The singers never turn up. But one of the guests produces a couple of bottles of chhang. And another has arranged for momoes, difficult to get in Leh after the boycott of Muslim butchers. Chhang and momoes are passed around in a ritual reminiscent of transubstantiation in reverse. Perhaps tourists do have their uses, toffees to Tara notwithstanding.

'Julay!' I say to the man behind the departure counter at Leh airport. 'Julay,' he responds equably. And surely it is only in my imagination that his bland expression seems to add, 'Don't you know it's October, you ignorant git?'

Camel Ahoy!

I'd have made a lousy Lawrence of Arabia. Ask Paploo. Paploo was the first—and I hope last—camel in my life. It was 1991, and I was on a desert safari in Rajasthan.

But if Paploo gave me a hard time, in the end I got my own back on him. Thanks to a creature even scarier than Paploo. A creature with wings...

I'd walk a mile for a camel—in the opposite direction. That was what I'd have liked even with Paploo. If he was going south, I would have liked to be bound for the north. That's what democracy is all about and it was fine for me. Except that I was supposed to be riding Paploo, an exercise that would have been facilitated considerably had the two of us been travelling towards more or less the same point of the compass. But camels, as I was beginning to learn, have a mind—and a method of locomotion—uniquely their own.

Till I had made the acquaintance of Paploo some hours earlier, camels had been for me ships of the desert that pass in the night, strictly non-union cast members strayed off the sets of a remake of *The Return of the Sheikh*. Now I was sitting on one, more or less (less more and more less) and feeling like laundry left over from *Lawrence of Arabia*.

I was on a camel trek along the fringe of the Rajasthan desert, billed as the definitive adventure experience ('Real Sand Safari for Rs 50 per day only ... fooding, experienced driver etc ... contact Aswin') for those who have seen and done it all already, from rafting in the Zanskar valley to taking a postprandial constitutional in the Hindu Kush. I haven't done either, but I had felt I could hack it. That was before I met the beast.

We had long left behind the tent city of Pushkar. A flyblown speck on the map, 160 kilometres from Jaipur, Pushkar buzzes to life on the first full-moon night in November when throngs of Hindu devotees from all over the country flock to take a pre-dawn dip in the village lake, considered sacred to Brahma.

The camel and cattle fair that coincides with the religious festival is considered sacred to Thomas Cook. Overnight, the desert blooms with the rainbow efflorescence of a thousand tents that spring out of the sand to house visitors. It is a high, wide, and handsome affair, of the kind that Rajasthan is so good at when it tilts back its colourful turban, gives an extra twist to its moustache, and gets down to the serious business of marketing ethnic exuberance.

Jazzy neon jinks in time to the strains of amplified Hindi pop blaring over the fairground. On a raised platform, a hermaphrodite in a tinsel sari does a Michael Jackson number to drum up customers for the lurid splendour of the 'Maruti Sarkus'. A dancer with seven water-pots balanced on his head twirls past a sign proclaiming 'Best spaghetti in Rajasthan—recommended by Italians!'

And everywhere there are Paploo-clones. Camels—smelling of ancient sofas left in the rain—undulate by, plastic flowers in their supercilious nostrils and paisley designs painted on their scrawny rumps like registration numbers on motor vehicles.

Rampal had sidled up to me with a seductive 'Psst! Cheap camel ride', while Paploo cocked an inviting eyebrow at me as though to say: 'Come on, make my day.' I had succumbed, and here I was on my camel odyssey, the rolling dunes stretching away to infinity.

The quietness was as tangible as the afternoon heat. Much more than the mere absence of sound, it was a vibrant element pregnant with metaphysical significance, a comma in the syntax of suspense. The suspense revolved around the question as to when Paploo and I would part company, unintentionally on my part. While some of Paploo moved clockwise, the remainder of him seemed simultaneously to move anticlockwise. It was like sitting astride a maverick mobile corkscrew. Every now and then, Paploo would detour and snake out a serpentine neck to help himself to hors d'oeuvres from a passing thorn bush, making our progress even more erratic.

'Say "Hat, hat, hat!" to him,' admonished Rampal, my friend, philosopher, and camel guide. I dutifully enunciated the mantra, without noticeable effect. 'Kick him in the ribs,' advised Rampal. This seemed a rash familiarity, but I essayed a tentative nudge with my heels.

Paploo broke wind comprehensively. At first I interpreted this to be an aid to propulsion—jet-age travel by camel class, so to speak. But it turned out to be no more than a general philosophical observation and we plodded on towards the dunes that seemed as distant as ever. I hung on grimly, steeling myself with the foreboding that the worst was yet to come.

An eternity later we reached the rendezvous where the car waited to take me back to civilization. With a final eructation, Paploo knelt and I tumbled into Rampal's waiting grasp. 'How was it?' he grinned wolfishly. 'It was nothing,' I replied lightly. 'Now I go to Jaipur where I am wait-listed to catch the indefinitely postponed Indian Airlines flight home.'

Rampal's face under his ten-gallon turban paled at the very mention of this ultimate, edge-of-the-brink safari to end all safaris. Even Paploo looked stricken. And as I drove away into the sunset I had the satisfaction of knowing that in recompense for my aching limbs I was leaving behind an aghast camel who, if ever we met again, would walk a mile for me—in the opposite direction.

The Seventeen-minute Saga

Rajasthan, ancient land of chivalry, is resonant with romance. I was witness to the birth of one such legend, backdropped by the splendour of Lake Pichola at sunset.

It was a timeless saga that had to be made in precisely seventeen minutes. And so it was. Thanks to the man from London. With a little help from a motley crowd of onlookers who had their own interpretations as to what the tamasha was all about.

The blood-red sun hung like a burnished shield over the crest of the Aravali hills, turning Lake Pichola into a sheet of crimson. Slanting sunbeams caught the jade-and-amber crystals topping the pinnacles of the palace on the lake—errant shooting stars from a turquoise sky. The towering ramparts on the bank glowed gold in the alchemy of light. Red and gold—apt hues to evoke the legend of Rajputana, Land of Kings, steeped in war and splendour and tales of Rajput valour as it defied Mughal might.

It was here that Maharana Udai Singh shifted his capital from embattled Chittor and, in 1559, founded Udaipur, the city named after him. A hard gallop away is the pass of Haldighat where, in 1576, the flower of Rajput chivalry led by Maharana Pratap Singh was cut down by Akbar's army under Man Singh. It is said that the sough of arrows was like wind through a field of corn and the clash of steel woke echoes in the distant hills.

But the man from London had things other than ancient battles, won or lost, on his mind. He was busy mounting his own campaign. 'Seventeen minutes,' he said. 'That's exactly how long the dusk lasts here at this time of year. I've timed it.'

And in seventeen minutes he had to capture the essence of his story which, in its way, was as much a contemporary romance as had been the sagas celebrated by minstrels in the far pavilions of the past. He was making an advertising film for an international brand of cigarettes. The story, like all good stories of all climes and ages, was simple. It featured the Man: tall, handsome, a patrician presence dominating boardroom or social rendezvous. The Woman: wife of the Man, beautiful, immaculately groomed, a charming consort to her husband. The Driver: spotlessly uniformed, loyal, a trusted family retainer. And, last but far from least, the Car: a gleaming symbol of power and success, worthy successor to Chetak, Rana Pratap's legendary steed.

The Car had posed daunting problems of logistics to get on location. Brought up from Bombay by a driver (not to be confused with the Driver) it had undergone several adventures, including an encounter with a wayward buffalo, before reaching Udaipur. Smarting under some imagined slight, the driver, who looked like an out-of-work Hindi-movie heavy, had turned bolshy and had been heard muttering vague but dire threats that caused the man from London to fear he would sabotage the Car, or the film, or both, given half a chance. Crew members had been alerted to keep a close eye on the malcontent.

But now everything was finally set. The cameras, perched in turrets where archers must once have crouched, were ready to roll.

The Car, with the Driver at the wheel and the Man and the Woman in the rear seat, was to be shown winding through country roads in the tawny twilight. Headlights blazing, it would roll down the incline in the dusk, to the jetty where a canopied boat waited. The Driver would open the rear door and the Man and the Woman would get into the boat, in which a hamper would also be placed. The boat would arc out to the illuminated Lake Palace, its silvery wake glowing in the gathering dark. The final shot would show the Man and the Woman, he in dinner jacket and smoking, she in evening gown and radiant, silhouetted against the last ember glow of sunset. Crescendo of music, fade out.

It was beautiful, it was effective, it was neat. It was designed to make you feel that if you had the good taste to smoke the cigarette being promoted, like the Man you too might find yourself with a lovely and loving companion, being driven around a picture-book landscape on the ritziest set of wheels this side of a punk-rock superstar's dreams. The tapestry of association was deftly woven, twining the silken strands of a resplendent past with the crush-proof texture of today.

Trouble was it had all to be wrapped up in seventeen minutes. Seventeen minutes might sound a lot for a sixty-second film. But takes, retakes, and re-retakes gobble up time. Of course, the sequence could be shot in instalments over several sunsets. But it was generally felt that if executed in one fine swoop the exercise could have a graceful spontaneity lacking in a piecemeal endeavour.

So seventeen minutes it was.

The job wasn't made any easier by a large and curious crowd that had collected to watch the shooting. Word had buzzed around the honeycomb of lanes in the old city, and fiercely moustached old men in huge white turbans, women in dazzlingly bright ghagras and blouses, balancing water pots on their heads, and children scampering like spinning tops had swarmed to the lakeside. Tourists, Indian and foreign, swelled the motley throng. Several vendors set up stalls selling tea and peanuts. A dhobi laden with bundles of laundry stopped to watch, and a man trundling a block of ice on a handcart parked his vehicle in a corner.

'How are we going to control this lot?' the man from London asked no one in particular.

The crowd hummed with conjecture and comment.

'Is that Sean Connery?' someone asked, spotting the Man and obviously thinking of *Octopussy* that had been filmed in Udaipur some time ago.

'No, no. It's a Hindi movie.'

'That does not sound like a Mercedes engine,' said a sceptical German voice, referring to the spluttering of the generator concealed in the boot of the Car to power the camera for close-ups when the vehicle was in motion.

'It's all an election gimmick, yaar.'

'Arre nahin, I tell you it's got something to do with family planning.'

'Please, get back! Get back, please! Lights! Action!' The man from London seemed everywhere and nowhere at once.

The floodlights blazed, the Car rolled down the slope, the camera whirred. The crowd fell silent, spellbound by the making of illusion. But what was real? The watching crowd, the glowing mirage of the palace on the water, the shades of the past beating like pigeons' wings in the thickening air?

Philosophical musings were jostled aside by slapstick as the tracking camera picked up the dhobi's bundles of laundry. The man from London shouted, 'Cut! Get those flaming things out of here.' A couple of crew members fell over themselves in a welter of haste and bed sheets to remove the offending objects.

The Car and the camera rolled again. The light sank like sand in the hourglass of dusk. The first stars spangled the indigo sky, vying to upstage the lights of the palace. The first shot was over.

The second shot was hurriedly set up: the Car on the quay, the boat and palace in the background. The models got out to stretch their legs while the lights and the camera were being positioned. 'Let's go,' said the man from London. The Driver opened the Car's door for the Woman. Suddenly, a figure reared up in the back seat like a malevolent jack-in-the-box. It was the mutinous driver who had taken the opportunity of the crew's distraction to lay claim to his dispossessed Car by sneaking into it for a quick lie-down. With the man from London snapping at his heels, he was herded from the set, shambling with sheepish villainy.

The camera rolled for the final shot. The Driver handed the Woman and the Man out of the Car and into the boat.

The boat curved away from the jetty towards the glittering palace, its wake a gleaming scimitar on the beaten silver of the lake. In the timeless hush before the curtain-fall of night, the puttering of its outboard engine might have been fading hoof-beats galloping into a happily-ever-after sunset.

The seventeen minutes were over.

The crowd, stirred with the sigh of night breeze, began to drift away, voices echoing on ancient stone.

'He was very handsome, no?'

'Yes, she was lovely.'

'You can't tell me that was a Mercedes engine.'

'Wish they'd asked some of us to join in. I wouldn't have minded at all.'

'What was it all about, anyway?'

In answer, the dhobi picked up his bundles and walked away, and the man with the handcart looked at the puddle where his ice had been and in which the lights on the quay were reflected in a Cheshire-cat smile.

Rites of Passage

In February 1991, we took the seven-day Palace on Wheels (POW) railway tour through Rajasthan. It was an historic trip, in more ways than one. The Gulf War broke out the morning after we began our journey. Which was to be the last journey of the old POW; the original railway coaches in which we travelled have been put into museums and replaced by modern, air-conditioned coaches. One up for comfort, two down for romance.

We had a ticketless passenger on board. Sawai Madho I of Jaipur. Called Sawai (one and a quarter) because according to folklore he was so large (seven feet, 500 lbs) that you could have made one and a quarter maharajahs out of him instead of just one.

On the new, sanitized POW, old SM, as I got to call him after our trip together, wouldn't have stood a ghost of a chance.

Sawai Madho Singh I, formerly of Jaipur, was not amused. All right, so his successors and other fellow princes have been derecognized since his elevation to an even higher sphere. But that's no excuse to expect him to cram his spectral bulk, all seven feet and 500 lbs of it, into a cabin which could do double duty as a waistcoat if they let out a couple of buttons. How's a fellow to breathe, let alone move, in this trim-fit casket? Call it a 'Palace on Wheels'? Heads should roll.

Squeezing past old Sawai Madho's ghostly dudgeon, I survey the tiny, two-bunk coupe that Bunny and I are going to travel in for seven days. It must, I reflect, have been pretty hard paneer being a maharajah. Or, for that matter, an avatar thereof in the form of a modern-day tourist bent on being taken for a royal ride down the tracks of history.

Outside, on the Delhi Cantonment platform, liveried staffers in red turbans are ushering garlanded passengers into the Palace on Wheels, which, in the initial stage of its 2400-km odyssey, will be pulled by the turn-of-the-century steam locomotive, the Desert Queen.

'Oh, my Gad!' wails a New World voice. 'They've got Indian showers in the bathroom!' Intrigued by what the voice obviously believes to be some ingenious form of indigenous torture, I peer into a pink-tiled bathroom equipped with a Western-style WC, wash basin, electric geyser. And a steel bucket and mug, presumably the 'showers' in anguished question. Beside me, SM gives vent to a wraith-like snort, but whether in amusement or indignation, I cannot tell.

Back in the lounge area provided in each coach (ours, CT-7, was built in the Ajmer workshop in 1911 for the viceroy, so what SM is doing as my self-appointed fellow-traveller I don't know, but there he is) the saloon captain, R.S. Tewari, and his assistant, Shiv Ram, introduce themselves with old-world courtesy. They will be looking after our needs for the duration of the journey. The one-km-long, metre-gauge train, Tewari explains, has twelve passenger saloons like ours, all built for regal VIPs in the mid-nineteenth century or early twentieth century. Each coach sleeps twelve passengers in two-berth and four-berth cabins. Each coach has two loos, a service area and a private lounge, done in period style. Of a total capacity of 100, the train is carrying eighty-six passengers, almost all foreigners. Not a bad payload, all things considered. Our coach has a Danish party of four, the Jansens; Vir and Rekha Rawlley; Bunny and myself. And, of course, SM.

Escorted to the dining saloon (tiny crystal chandeliers, silken napery, red carpet) we are given an excellently cooked and immaculately served meal of Indian and Western fare, which somewhat mollifies SM. Back in CT-7, Bunny opts for the bottom bunk, so I take the top, even narrower. POW begins to roll. And sway. And pitch. And roll some more. I drift into uneasy sleep, am startled awake by a violent shudder. Is it a stray Scud strike from the Gulf War, or an errant B-52? No—only SM turning over in phantom repose. I fall back into fitful slumber.

Day Two

Jaipur. Tewari asks if we slept well. SM and I growl disclaimers in chorus. But at the entrance there are caparisoned elephants salaaming welcome with their trunks, more garlands, wailing shehnais, whining sarangis, all effectively drowning out the busybody fiddling with a transistor blathering about some war, somewhere.

We board a sightseeing bus. Anil Malik, the affably energetic senior manager who has been with POW since its inception in the early 1980s, bids us welcome. POW, he says, is not about luxury; POW is about history. And history often proves to be a bumpy ride, a memorable but less than entirely comfortable rite of passage. SM nods in lugubrious agreement.

With clockwork precision we are whisked through the sights: Hawa Mahal, City Palace, Amber Fort, Nahargarh. Then it's back to POW—where Shiv Ram waits to pour us a nightcap and ask after our day—and to the realization that sometimes the journey is the destination, that to travel historically is better than to arrive.

Not even SM's snores can wake me that night.

Day Three

Chittorgarh. Sunlight on a broken column. Weathered stone that bore blind witness to Padmini's beauty which, reflected in a mirror, maddened Alauddin Khilji and led to the destruction of the citadel. War and repentance in a Polaroid snapshot. SM shakes his head sepulchrally at the slings and arrows of outrageous Eros.

Romance, uncrossed by stars or adverse signals, also blossoms on POW. Anil Malik tells us of two young American passengers who, carried away by the staccato serenade of the steel tracks, exchanged moonlit rings at the Taj Mahal and married each other shortly thereafter.

This time around too, there is romance in the air. Maria Louisa seems to be carrying a torch for saloon captain Tewari, and blows him flying kisses across the length of the lounge, much to the amusement of her parents and the consternation of SM who does not approve of such forward behaviour. However, there is no imminent expectation of wedding bells ringing again, thanks to POW. For one thing, Tewari is already happily married. For another, Maria Louisa has yet to celebrate her fourth birthday.

But two impromptu birthday parties do take place on board, amidst a polyglot chorus of congratulations around the cakes presented with compliments of the management. SM joins in the celebratory sing-song in a horrendous French accent. I fear he is catching the infection of cosmopolitan camaraderie which is doing the rounds.

Day Four

Udaipur. The Lake Palace Hotel glinting like a jewel set on the burnished steel of Lake Pichola. Not far away is Haldighat. The silent hills still resound with the legends of Rana Pratap.

The guide explains that the Udaipur rulers called themselves maharanas, a cut above maharajahs, not to mention lowly rajas. In a huff, SM stalks off to read about his own family history in the comfortable library attached to the elegantly appointed lounge-cum-bar on POW.

The whistle blows and we are on the move again through an increasingly arid landscape. Desert dust trickles in, parching throats and keeping the bartender busy. SM raises an ironic eyebrow at such effeteness. Venture across the wastes of history and yet jib at the sands of time? Forsooth!

Day Five

Jaisalmer. The fort rising like a golden mirage out of the desert. A copperplate script of camels etched against a blood-red sun. The old havelis veiled in carved stone as delicate as a fall of lace.

And in the evening, flickering bonfires illuminate Rajasthani folk dances in which everyone joins, egged on by POW manager Emmanuel Johnson. SM leads the conga line, foot-stomping and hand-clapping with the best of them, as though to the disco born. Maybe this new-fangled democracy business has its points after all.

Day Six

Jodhpur. The brooding hulk of Mehrangarh Fort, its craggy face pocked with the ancient cicatrix of cannon fire. The sprawl of the town far below, like a dizzy throw of blue-tinted dice. The echoing coolness of Umaid Bhawan Palace with its feast of princely memorabilia and equally lavish buffet lunch, of which SM has three helpings. All this and haggling for handicrafts too. At only US $130 per pax per day? Cheap at the price. Even for mere mortals and other commoners.

Day Seven

Bharatpur bird sanctuary, followed by Fatehpur Sikri, Akbar's dream city that had everything but water, a lack which caused him to desert it a scant seven years after it was founded. Then Agra and the Taj Mahal. Because it is there; the ultimate picture-postcard, entrancing monument to monstrous egotism.

We stay on board, to be taken for a guided tour of POW by SM. All the coaches are equally splendid but some are more equal than others. Like the resplendent Bikaner Saloon, for instance, as SM grumpily admits. He cheers up a bit, however, when we assure him that the two Jaipur coaches are almost as nice.

There is a wistful air of valediction. For soon, not only will we be bidding farewell to POW, but the train itself will be taking its last bow. When this season ends, come the end of March, the old POW will be replaced by a new, streamlined, air-conditioned, dust-free version, currently being built in Madras. It is hoped that the updated POW, which will continue to be run by the Rajasthan Tourism Development Corporation, will extend the current schedule of twenty-six weekly round trips between October and March. The new train will certainly be more comfortable. But it is doubtful if it will accommodate insubstantial excess baggage in the ghostly form of SM.

As we get down at Delhi, I hear a resigned sigh behind us. We turn to look, but it's only the Desert Queen emitting a last puff of steam.

An Island Called Piety

*Bunny and I first went to Goa in 1982. We've been back
several times since. Each time we visit we notice changes,
most not for the better. Vindaloo and sorpotel displaced by
Sher-e-Punjab tandoori chicken; homemade feni by mass-
produced Bagpiper; the Portuguese fado with Daler Mehndi.*

*But despite these changes, there's an essence about the
place which remains changeless. Perhaps it's because, as this
piece suggests, Goa is an island in the stream of time.*

Mario Cabral e Sa of Piedade. We had the name and
address all right. But how do you find a fable? It might
as easily have been Don Quixote de la Mancha we were
looking for. Or Sir Lancelot du Lac, sometime of Camelot.
Myths don't come with a map and convenient postal code.

Not that there had been anything elusive or insubstantial
about Mario when we finally met and had a feni together in
the sleepy little roadside taverna outside Panjim. The green-
gold Goan afternoon shrouded around us in a siesta hush
punctuated by the clucking of unseen hens and the buzz of
flies the duenna behind the bar swatted in her sleep.

'Come and see me sometime on Piedade,' said Mario, burly
and bearded. 'It's an island on the Mandovi River and its name
means "piety". It's where I live.' And grinning hugely at this
improbable juxtaposition, he downed his feni like a draught
of sacramental wine. We eagerly accepted the invitation. Mario
was a well-known journalist and an expert on his native Goa.

Goa's liberation in 1961 was followed by an invasion of
tourists, including latter-day hippies on the rebound from

the Kathmandu trail. With its laid-back lifestyle and hothouse lushness incorporating the surf-and-sand trimmings obligatory for all tropical paradises, Goa is ideal vacation land—perhaps too ideal.

Having done the round of quaint little churches and quainter tavernas, eaten the searing vindaloo and drunk the fiery cashew-nut feni, listened to the haunting fado, and unskinny-dipped at Calangute, we wanted for a while to be real people again and see what other real people did, whatever that might be, when they weren't humouring visitors by doing what the travel brochures said they were supposed to.

Piedade sounded like the answer.

It's been said there is something erotic about islands. An echo perhaps of castaway adolescence, Miranda pursued by Caliban, or an even earlier Garden of Innocence yet to be lost. Eros or no, islands are fascinating bubbles in the river of time.

So we went in search of Piedade, unannounced, there being no phones on the island. As Mario had instructed, we waved down a rattletrap country bus crammed with vegetable vendors, squalling babies in arms, girls carrying squawking chickens in baskets, and little old ladies in black who looked like everyone's grandmothers ought to. Helpful hands squeezed us aboard and the bus rolled off, barrelling down the green tunnel of road bordered by a wall of vegetation that occasionally revealed a tumble-down villa.

We got off at the brooding, jungle-cloaked ruins of Vella Goa, the old, deserted capital, and walked past the Cathedral of Bom Jesu. Down an overgrown path was the broad muddy sweep of the Mandovi, on the bank of which, miraculously, was a tiny landing stage, just as Mario had said there would be.

A small group of people and assorted livestock waited by the jetty. The passengers seemed to be peasants, plainly but neatly dressed for the outing. We were greeted by a nod or two of acknowledgement but no open curiosity. Islands breed their own reticence. I pointed to a green smudge on the river, shimmering in the heat haze.

'Piedade?'
'Piedade!'

That ended the conversation, for our co-passengers spoke nothing but a mixture of Konkani and Portuguese, a dialect as spicy as pork sorpotel and based on a recipe as difficult to learn.

Presently, a rusty old tin tub drew up, its engine missing a beat in every three. Animals and people got out, animals and people got in, in that order. Piedadians, I was beginning to learn, have their priorities right. A person is a person, but a good goat is a potential xacuti, the popular Goan stew thickened with coconut milk.

The overloaded ark moved out onto the Mandovi, thumping engine in imminent danger of cardiac arrest. But Piedade looks after its own, and in a surprisingly short time we reached our destination.

But where had we reached? A pier, a derelict shack, a road running past in both directions, undulating fields beyond like a painted backdrop for a pastoral play. Our co-passengers seemed to dematerialize instantly the moment they stepped onto home soil, all except two massive matrons dressed in the mandatory black. We stood flat-footed, strangers in an un-signposted paradise. Mario hadn't said what we were to do next.

Out of nowhere, a three-wheeler scooter taxi puttered up. The matrons squeezed themselves into the single passenger seat. One of them beckoned us over. In the colloquy that followed, the word 'Mario'—used with varying intonations of query and affirmation—emerged as the sole point of mutual comprehension.

A rapid-fire exchange took place between the two passengers and the driver. A decision having been reached, one of the matrons indicated we squeeze onto their laps. Mumbled protests cut short by a sharp command and a sharper tug on the arm, we found ourselves gingerly perched on ample black skirts. The three-wheeler spluttered off with its strangely assorted cargo, me bleakly wondering how I get into these things and my two co-passengers carrying on an animated conversation between themselves as if riding along with total strangers on your lap was the most natural thing in the world.

And perhaps on Piedade it was. There was a comfortable unselfconsciousness about the cotton-candy clouds drifting across the blue sky, the languid sun dappling the chequerboard of paddy fields and the encircling frieze of palm trees. Winsome as it was, Piedade gave the impression that looking good wasn't its most important occupation—that you'd be ill-advised to try and get it to pose for your camera. At least that's what I told myself when I discovered that, inevitably, I had forgotten to load my battered Pentax.

Except for our three-wheeler and a bus that passed us with a toot of its horn, there was no other motor traffic on the road. The occasional cyclist or pedestrian waved in reflex, assured that on their island there could be no one they didn't know.

In the afternoon sun, the landscape seemed to need nothing more than a simple alchemy of light and air and water to burgeon green and ripe.

We trundled into a tiny village: a whitewashed church, a couple of tavernas and a huddle of tiled-roof houses shawled in lacy bougainvillea. Our co-passengers paid their part of the fare and bustled away. The driver held up four fingers to indicate we owed him four rupees as our share for the ride. Then sensing our anxiety he reassuringly said 'Mario' several times, collared a passing boy who was rolling along the lid of a tin can with a stick, gave instructions, and gestured that we follow him.

Our clattering progress down the street attracted some curiosity, which our guide satisfied with cheery cries of 'Casa Mario!' Soon he stopped and indicated that he wasn't going our way any more. But we were in safe hands. The bush telegraph that crackles in the ether of every tightly knit community had picked up the news that there were visitors from the outside world to see Mario and we were passed on with gestured directions from back garden to tiny back garden, in a rite of passage usually reserved for nothing more substantial than a scrap of threadbare gossip.

'Casa Mario!' said our last cicerone with a flourish, and we had arrived.

A stone house, large by village standards, rooted in place like an ancient oak. A knock on the polished wooden door admitted us into a cool, lofty interior, stone flagged, sparsely but elegantly furnished with straight-backed chairs and round tables. The steep angle of light slanting in from the windows reminded me of a Vermeer painting.

The lady who had let us in introduced herself as Mario's wife, and in halting English regretted that her husband was away. Seeing our disappointment, she insisted we sit and left the room to return with a taller, younger version of Mario, beard and all, obviously his son.

Over strong, sweet coffee, Mario's son, Nandu, in fluent English flecked with irony, told us about the life and times of the island.

Piedade, where their family had been for longer than anyone cared to remember, was approximately seven kilometres long and a little less than three kilometres wide. There were two villages, situated at either end and connected by the island's single road. There were less than six privately owned cars on Piedade, one bus which shuttled between the two villages, and two scooter taxis, one of which we had travelled by. There was no petrol pump on Piedade, no movie hall, no hospital, no bank. So almost everything had to be shipped across by ferry, including education, there being no high school either.

Piedade also did not have a police station. Whether as a cause or effect of this, there was no crime on the island. Local lore had it that once, many years ago, a robbery had taken place. But since the robbers, like everyone else, had to wait for the ferry to get off the island, they had been rounded up easily and persuaded to see the folly of their ways.

Having asked to be excused, I was directed to a vast, airy room dominated by two huge throne-like chairs with hinged

seats. Through the open window came a faint snorting of
pigs. Conventional plumbing it might lack, but Piedade made
its own sanitary arrangements.

Nandu offered to show us around the island and we set
off in the family car, a new model Ambassador, itself
something of a curiosity on Piedade.

The small houses, with steep roofs and verandahs,
crowded together like gossipy old women, faces hidden by
the lacy fans of flowering creepers. Many of them had wreaths
of grass and ribbons hanging outside. 'Anti-hex signs,' said
our guide, 'to avert the evil eye.' Security measures, after all,
need not begin or end with burglar alarms and guard dogs.

A house, ostensibly no different from its neighbours, was
pointed out to us as a local landmark. It belonged to the
family that started the Indian version of the Old Spice range
of cosmetics. If anything, it made the outside world seem
even more remote.

We drove along the single, straight road into the other
village, and up an incline to a church we were told was built
in the sixteenth century. A film crew from Bombay had visited
the place a few days ago and the children were still in a welter
of excitement about it. The sight of my camera produced
whoops and cheers, it being taken for granted that I too had
something to do with the silver screen. One by one, they
trooped up to have their pictures taken, irrepressible delight
bubbling through the solemn formality of their poses. The
fact that I was clicking an empty camera did not mar the
mutual enjoyment in the slightest.

Visitors, we were told, particularly camera-clad ones who
might have something to do with magical moviedom, were a
highly prized commodity on Piedade. It was practically the
civic duty of the host to take visitors around so that everyone
could get a good look at them and thus ensure a common
subject for conversation for at least the next fortnight.

With the shadows lengthening, our hosts said they would
drop us back at the ferry landing. Bidding them goodbye, we
told them they were living in a paradise and that we envied

them. We wished we could live on Piedade. They laughed and said we would be bored out of our minds within a week, stuck in a place where there was nothing to do but gossip and grow vegetables and wait for the ferry to bring murmurs of happenings in the faraway world. We protested, saying we would love to lead such a life.

But we knew, and they knew, we were only being polite. Without doubt they were quite right. We would feel stagnant and get hopelessly bored without the gritty stimuli of city life, without the jostle and bustle of crowds and events and crises. But we also suspected that the failing would be not so much on Piedade's part as on ours.

That was nine years ago. I've never been back to Piedade, but I think of it often and wonder if it is greatly changed. It seems unlikely, but I'll never know for sure. For, of course, I shan't ever go back to Piedade again. You don't set out a second time for a fable already found, and lost.

Kerala in a Coconut

Before we went there in 1995, all that I knew about Kerala was that it was the first place in the world to have a democratically elected communist government (1959) and that Malayalam was a palindrome, being spelt the same front to back and back to front.

But it was only after we got there that I got to grips with Kerala's great coconut mystery ...

Kovalam is the Mona Lisa of beaches—too famous for its own good. After all that you've heard about it, when you actually see it you run the risk of initial anti-climax. Matters are not helped by the fact that the signboard which says Kovalam Beach points to the wrong beach. We follow the sign and come to a thin strip of boulder-strewn sand where the sea hisses and spits at us like an angry tomcat. 'Must be because of the monsoon; must be nicer in season,' I mutter. 'Must be,' Bunny concurs dubiously. We trudge back to the fork and take the other road which is signposted Lighthouse Beach. Round a rocky headland, two perfect scallops of beach open up in front of us, fringed by palm trees and souvenir stalls selling 'Son of a Beach' T-shirts. A smorgasbord of open-air eateries offer 'you buy, we fry' freshly caught seafood. This is more like the Kovalam of picture-postcard fame. The surf purrs like a kitten.

'Seafood wanting?' A young man, dhoti worn at half mast in true Malayali fashion, asks us in 'touristese', the local lingua franca.

'Wanting,' we agree, and he leads us to a thatch-roofed shack. While the fish is frying, I ask for a drink: 'Two coconut bringing, please.'

Our host nods vigorously in negation. 'Pepsi bringing!' he beams.

'Coconut bringing,' I correct him.

'Beer bringing!' he counters.

'Coconut,' I reiterate.

'Dollar changing?' he asks eagerly, in a ploy to throw me off this coconut fetish.

'No dollar changing; coconut bringing—now!' I admonish sternly.

'Coconut cannot bringing,' he says glumly.

'Why cannot bringing?' I ask, pointing to the literally thousands of coconut trees, each laden with fruit, that surround us.

'Climbing man gone,' replies our host, as though to say: You know what these mod cons are like; you can never depend on them, and the after-sales service is lousy.

'Why can't you climb the tree?' I ask, losing my 'touristese' for the moment.

Our host looks horrified, as though I had made an indecent proposal. 'I, management; climbing man, climbing man,' he says. 'Management cannot climbing.'

So Bunny and I settle for Pepsis and learn our first lesson about Kerala.

The supple mudra of the coconut palm as it caresses the sky is an eloquent symbol of Kerala. Surging out of the bountiful earth, the kalpaka groves represent the spirit of the land, its creative zest and its generous hospitality. The coconut is Kerala's Kalpataru, supplier of all that the heart desires. It provides condiment and cooking medium, votive offering and ceremonial accessory, building material and decorative gewgaw. It is central to the economy. Alleppey is said to be the biggest coconut market in the world, with the next three years' crop sold out in advance. Yet try to buy a single green coconut to drink in Kerala. Chances are you'll hear the same refrain we did: 'Yes, we have no coconuts today.'

Perhaps because of its inestimable value in its generic totality, an individual coconut is literally priceless, and therefore un-sellable. Who would want to buy it and why and for how much? There could be another reason, one that reveals more about the Keralite than about the coconut. And that reason may lie in the Malayali's passionate belief in his progressiveness, a capacity which has enabled him to escape the clutch of customary circumstance to embrace the new and the unexplored.

Passion, of course, is the core of the Malayali being. To the Malayali it doesn't seem to matter so much what you do or don't do, just so long as you are passionate about it. So he is passionate about faith and he is passionate about scepticism; he is passionate about communism and he is passionate about petro-dollar capitalism; he is passionate about indulgence and he is passionate about abstinence. Which is why, in Kerala you might see a lot of religion but not too much religiosity; ideology but not necessarily indoctrination; a lot of drinking but little drunkenness. Such cultural cross-currents give the Malayali his innate dynamism.

The Malayali's get-up-and-go has chalked up a number of firsts for his part of the world. The first part of the country to conduct foreign trade, long before the advent of Vasco da Gama. The first to rise in rebellion against foreign rule. The first to have a family planning programme. The first state in India to achieve a hundred per cent literacy.

Not satisfied with all these landmarks of progress, the Malayali continues to pursue the progressive, so much so that often he progresses himself right out of where he comes from. This is not difficult to do. Kerala is a small state, comprising only 1.03 per cent of India's total land area. Densely packed, it does not have the traditional divide between town and town or between town and country; one seems to flow into the other. So if you have someone going to Thiruvananthapuram and he is asked where he is going, by the time he replies Thiruvananthapuram he'll probably not only have reached Thiruvananthapuram, but left it behind, and be in Kottayam instead, and by the time he has corrected himself, he is no longer in Kottayam but in Kozhikode.

This baffling velocity is aided and abetted not only by the fact that most places in Kerala have two names, the new and the old, like Thiruvananthapuram and Trivandrum, but also by the Malayali capacity to introduce more syllables, consonants and vowels into them than they intrinsically possess. Malayalis are passionately proud of Malayalam and rightly so, and make all their place names and descriptions sound like stanzas of epic poetry. Thus Kerala—spelt Kay-Yee-Yar-Yay-Yel-Yay—becomes Kairralluh, and the sobriquet of Alleppey or Allapuzha, the Venice of the East, becomes Thee Venniss of thee Yeastuh, spelt Yee-Yay-Yes-Tee. And by the time you have got that all figured and spelt out you have left behind not only Kozhikode which is also Calicut but also Kannur which is also Cannanore and are now in some place called Delhi, or Dubai, or Dallas, or whatever, where you might as well set up shop and become an award-winning novelist like Arundhati Roy, or a cartoonist and designer like Ravi Shankar, or a newspaper editor like B.G. Verghese, or an advertising tycoon like George John, or the dudhwala of the nation like Verghese Kurien. Which is why finding a Keralite in Kerala is almost as difficult as finding a coconut. But then, that's the price of Malayali progressiveness.

Journeying through Kerala, the visitor from the north is forcefully struck by the many differences in both the physical and the cultural landscape from what he is used to. The south, and Kerala in particular, seems to belong not just to a different world but to a different civilizational order. Just as there are few sharp schisms between urban and rural, the divisions between wealth and want are less clearly demarcated. True, opulent villas done up in Gulf Gothic periodically peer out of the foliage, cheek by jowl with humble cottages and shacks.

But to compensate, women bearing loads on their heads routinely sport gold watches. Begging is non-existent, except in the immediate vicinity of places of worship where the mendicants seem to seek alms less for the sake of the money than out of a sense of public service to pilgrims who might wish to exercise the spiritual sinews of charity.

Children carry books in Kerala. Not, as they do in the north, to help strengthen their back muscles but in order to perform a strange ritual called reading. Weird, these Malloos. Everything seems remarkably clean, even in the bazaar areas. The result: no flies, despite the monsoon humidity. Market stalls and eateries sponsor a commendable spirit of culinary secularism with beef often on offer side by side with vegetarian fare. No one turns a hair, or a trishul. At regular intervals, neatly lettered signs announce licensed arrack and toddy shops. There is also a generous sprinkling of the beer parlours run by the Kerala Tourism Development Corporation. Pity there's so little dust on the road. I'd welcome the excuse to wet my throat.

We reach Alleppey and board a motorboat to take us via the celebrated backwaters to Chengacheri, three meandering hours away. As we putter through the emerald labyrinth of the backwaters we realize how inadequate the word 'green' is. How can one word describe so many variations on its theme? There is the joyous green of the palm fronds that intertwine overhead like the shy hands of young lovers, and the golden green of the sunlight dappling the jade green of the canal, which contrasts with the moss green of the log that bobs in the still water which reflects the bilious green of my face as I discover that the log is not a log but a dead dog.

We drive on to the Kumarakom bird sanctuary, at the edge of which is the Coconut Lagoon, run by the Casino group of hotels. A Heritage property, the resort has thirty-seven units made of components of traditional houses from all over Kerala which were dismantled, the individual pieces numbered, and reassembled on site. The bathrooms, equipped with all mod cons, are open air—a salubrious innovation.

Lunch is served in the dining unit, a 300-year-old house which once belonged to E.M.S. Namboodiripad's mother-in-law. This pinch of Marxist masala adds relish to the lavish buffet.

Driving through Kerala is a unique experience. The roads are generally good, but narrow and crowded. The drivers are as aggressive as those in north India, but display far greater finesse. In the split second before head-on collision, the opposing juggernauts dematerialize and re-materialize once the danger is past in a remarkable demonstration of mind over motor.

Such feats of mental legerdemain are made possible by the fact that the south Indian, particularly if he happens to hail from Kerala, has far greater brainpower than his counterpart in the north. Further evidence of this is supplied by a characteristic peculiar to the south Indian: while the rest of the world and its north-Indian brother nod their heads up and down to signify 'yes', and shake them from side to side to mean 'no', the south Indian does it the other way round. This single trait has ensured his evolutionary ascendancy over the rest of humankind. It is a simple matter of Darwinian selection: the principle of the survival of the fittest is far more likely to favour a species which, when it says 'no', makes it a point to do so in a way which enables it to keep an eye on its potential adversary from head to toe and thus accurately gauge the latter's size and possibly hostile reactions rather than a species which says 'no' by turning its head from side to side, thus taking its eye off the other fellow and doubling the risk of getting clobbered. Right? Shake your head if you agree.

We reach Thekkady, where the word 'teak' comes from. From a motorboat, we get distant views of wild elephant, bison, and deer. We get a closer view of the bed Rajiv Gandhi slept on in the Lake Palace, once owned by the raja of Travancore, and now run by the KTDC as a hotel. We move on to Munnar, where Kerala's tea comes from. Munnar has become a prime location for Hindi film shoots. If you mentally substitute heather and gorse for tea bushes in the misting drizzle, you could be in the Scottish highlands, no questions asked.

We come to Cochin. Dispersed over several islands and waterfronts linked by ferry, the composite city of Ernakulam-Cochin is reflective of Kerala's eclectic cultural mosaic. We stay on Bolghatty Island, in the KTDC's Bolghatty Palace Hotel. Built by the Dutch in 1744 as the governor's residence, it is still a magnificent building, PWD trappings notwithstanding. We visit Mattancharry Palace, built by the Portuguese in 1568 as a gift to the Cochin raja. Luminous murals tell the story of the Ramayana. Close by is the Jewish synagogue, dating back to 1568. The elegant webs of the Chinese fishing nets introduced by Kublai Khan's mariners festoon the approach to Fort Cochin. We visit St Francis Church, the oldest European church in India, where Vasco da Gama was buried for fourteen years before his relatives had his remains removed to Portugal.

On Willingdon Island we go to the Hotel Casino's seafood restaurant, said to be the best in the country. There is no fixed bill of fare, the 'menu' being a large trolley on which is displayed the catch of the day. The maitre d' prepares two enormous mixed platters for us, complete with Kerala's speciality, karimeen fish. He knows we'll never be able to finish them. We make a valiant effort. I raise a toast to Kerala. The tourist brochures call it God's own country. I drink to that. And I am grateful that, being a good Malayali, God has moved on to foreign parts to better His prospects, leaving His unattended bounty for interlopers like me to enjoy. Thank heaven for absentee landlordism, and pass me the rest of the karimeen.

AWAY

Island of the Day Before

Bunny and I went to Bali in 1996—if 1996, or any other calendar year, can be ascribed to the timeless enchantment of the island. The term 'earthly paradise' is often loosely used. Perhaps Bali comes closest to fitting this overused tag.

All good paradises must have a serpent in order to qualify as paradise. When we went there, Bali's resident serpent was called Mick. And he came in the guise of a timeshare holiday resort salesman with a Cockney accent. Read on ...

Jawaharlal Nehru called Bali 'the morning of the world'. When Bunny and I got there it sounded like the morning of the night before. Our jet-lagged senses, reeling after the eight-hour flight from Delhi, went into a tailspin by the barrage of French, German, Japanese, Dutch, Australian, and American that greeted us on arrival. We were guests of Club Mediterranee, popularly known as Club Med, the international resort chain. Begun in the 1950s in France, Club Med introduced a new concept in travel. It enabled the holidaymaker to go foreign without fears, enjoy the exotic without the angst. The concept seems to work. Today there are eighty Club Med resorts in thirty-five countries. Club Med Bali, on Nusa Dua beach, is typical.

We were greeted with floral garlands and escorted through lush coconut groves to our room, done in Balinese chic with central A/C and all other five-star mod cons. With one exception: no TV. The omission is deliberate. Club Med wants you to get out of boxes, including the box of your mind. Each Club Med resort is run like a village community comprising GMs (Gentle

Members, which means you) and GOs (Gentle Organizers). The GMs are encouraged by the GOs to participate in the many activities packed into the daily agenda. These include water sports like wind sailing and kayaking, golf on a six-hole course, archery, aerobics, disco dancing, silk-painting lessons, trapeze instructions, beer-drinking competitions, pillow-fight matches, and war cry yelling contests.

All this is part of the prepaid package and free of further cost to GMs. So is the food, laid on in lavish spreads in the main dining room and in two speciality restaurants, one serving seafood and the other Italian cuisine. Beer, wine, and soft drinks are on the house, in keeping with the Club Med philosophy of holidays without wallets. The only thing you pay for is drinks at the bar. Even here, no money changes hands, only bar beads which GMs can wear like tribal necklaces and keep unstringing in exchange for refreshment as they go along.

Discotheques? Trapeze acts? War cries? Bar beads? This sounds more like Saturday night fever in Karol Bagh, Delhi, than the morning of the world in Bali, Indonesia. What the heck happened to local culture? I demanded of a GO. There's plenty of that too, the GO assured me. Club Med organizes regular Balinese dance performances, and franchise shops on the premises sell local batiks, wood carvings, silk paintings, and jewellery. Haggle, advised the GO, gently. That's also part of local culture.

The next day we set out to explore Bali and discovered that while it was advisable to bargain for individual items, the island itself was a steal, an extravagantly bounteous gift of the gods to mere mortals. One of the 13,000 islands that constitute the Indonesian archipelago, Bali is a green bubble in the wake of its much larger neighbour, Java. Before the dawn of cliché, Bali took out a patent on that much-touted phrase: tropical island paradise.

Bali is paradise plus. For it represents not the fall of man but his continuing attempt to embellish his environment, as is the duty of every good tenant. Nature and artefact vie with each other, making the visitor catch his breath. The spectacular sunrise seems to flush scarlet and gold in astonishment at the batik artist's skill in ensnaring the miracle of colour on mundane cloth. Painted wooden demons and garudas mock the blue skies from which they have stolen the unravelled rainbows of their hues. The legong dancer's arched fingers echo the eloquent vibrancy of the wings of a hovering hummingbird. Intricately carved stone gateways guarded by droll stone gnomes erupt out of the soil like the petrified lava flow of Gunung Agung, the 10,000-foot extinct volcano on whose lower slopes nestles the Besakih temple, consecrated to the trinity of Brahma, Vishnu, and Shiva.

Legend has it that in the dawn of creation, so much beauty went into the making of Bali that the competing elements were about to explode. To save Bali, the gods scooped Gunung Agung out of the ocean floor and set it on the island like a giant paperweight to restore harmony and keep Bali safely moored to earth. A more prosaic view has it that Bali's cultural efflorescence is a result of the Mojopahit Hindu migration to the island in the fourteenth and fifteenth centuries, following the rising tide of Islam which was to sweep the archipelago. The court painters, dancers, and musicians were largely Hindu, and Bali became a haven of the arts. The Ramayana, and to a lesser extent the Mahabharata, remain the sources of inspiration for all Balinese art.

Bali's Hinduism is far different from that which is advocated by L.K. Advani and his followers. To the Balinese, Hinduism is not a political weapon but a celebration of life with all its joys and sorrows. It is, literally, a work of everyday art. It permeates everything, from the daily prasad of fruit and flowers offered in every home to the deities, to the kecak dance, depicting Sita's abduction by Ravana and her rescue by Rama, and which is unique in that no musical instruments are used, the accompaniment being provided by the male chorus going 'chak, chak, chak', in uncanny rhythm.

But like all sensible paradises, Bali recognizes that—like light without shadow, or like the silk of the rose without the sting of the thorn—good is meaningless without its opposite.

The mystical barong dance, in which entranced performers enact the struggle of good and evil, represents this moral chiaroscuro which relieves life from monochromatic monotony. On a more humdrum level, the same lesson is taught by Kuta beach. Called Surf City by Australian beachniks, Kuta is the most commercialized part of Bali.

At Kuta, Balinese women hawking 'I Love Bali' T-shirts and other touristy junk sidled up to us and crooned their wheedling chant: Where goo, where chee! Fee dolla, fee dolla! So chee, so chee! You buy, aye loo! (Very good, very cheap. Three dollars, three dollars. So cheap, so cheap. You buy, I lose.)

Fleeing from them, we bumped into a tout who asked me to pull a lucky number from an envelope. No payment, no obligation. Where goo! he beamed at me. You win firpri! Too towsan fie hunna dolla! (First prize. Two thousand five hundred dollars.) He led us into a nearby office to claim my prize. The makeshift office was crowded with an international assemblage of salespeople and apparent customers, all talking volubly. Our salesperson introduced himself as Mick and had an East London accent. Sab tikh hai! he greeted me in pidgin Hindustani to reassure me that he was familiar with my origins and customs. Mick wanted me to buy—right now, chance of a lifetime, mate!—a timeshare holiday scheme in Goa. He would give me a special 2500-dollar discount. That was the first prize I had won. But I had to put down a deposit right then. I shook my head and Mick's affability suddenly turned hostile. Bunny and I extricated ourselves from the ticklish situation.

As we walked away from the hard-sell clamour of Kuta, Bunny sighed and said that one had to accept that even paradise must have serpents in it in order to make it paradise. I agreed, but reserved a secret suspicion. What if Mick was not a bona fide serpent at all but was merely masquerading as one in order to impart a last fillip of excitement to our visit? It was possible. In the island Eden that is Bali, anything is possible, thanks to the special attention given to it by its very own resident GO called God.

Tibet: Land of an Eloquent Absence

I went to Tibet in 1994, under false pretences. When I applied for a Tibetan visa in Kathmandu, the Chinese authorities turned me down. The reason? I had an Indian passport, which said 'journalist' under the entry for 'Occupation'.

My contacts in Kathmandu advised me to get another passport. And friends in the ministry of external affairs and the regional passport office in Delhi obliged. I got a new passport, which did not have an entry for 'Occupation'.

'If anyone in Tibet asks you, remember to say you're a businessman. For God's sake don't let it slip you're a journalist or you could get into serious trouble. Safe journey and see you soon,' said my Kathmandu contacts, waving me off to my China Airways flight to Lhasa.

I waved back. And hoped they were right about the safe journey, and about seeing me back soon.

They say if you haven't karaoke-d in Lhasa you haven't karaoke-d at all. Garish neon advertises karaoke clubs and disco halls under the towering bastion of the Potala, the thirteen-storey winter palace of the Dalai Lama, which today looks like an exotic curio in someone else's living room. With its wide, potholed streets, raucous minibuses, juggling cycle-rickshaws, and square-shouldered buildings cloaked in the drab tunic of concrete, Lhasa is largely a post-Mao provincial Chinese city, with showcase American trimmings. The 468-room Lhasa Holiday Inn provides in-house oxygen on demand to combat the effects of being 12,000 feet above sea level and the Hard Yak Cafe bills itself as the 'Home of the Giant Yak-burger'. In Altitudes, 'the highest pub in the world', a Chinese duo croons Western pop music under the approving gaze of a pantheon of Hollywood icons, including James Dean, Marilyn Monroe, Clark Gable, and Greta Garbo. Giant sun umbrellas bearing the Marlboro legend flank the perspective of the 1300-year-old Jokhang temple which Buddhist pilgrims circumambulate in ritual prostration, braving the trampling feet of tourists and shoppers buying fake turquoise and smuggled second-hand US-aid clothes from Han Chinese stall keepers.

Is this really Tibet—the mystical Roof of the World, the Forbidden Land, the ultimate destination for the indomitable traveller? It isn't, and it is. For, like a palimpsest imperfectly erased, the real Tibet can be glimpsed as a fugitive vision behind the obscuring imprint of progressive Sinoization and the Four Modernizations.

I get my first glimpse of this alternate Tibet as our Toyota Runner speeds along the new highway that links the airport at Gonggar to Lhasa, ninety-six kilometres away. Along the course of the Lhasa River, the valley is fertile with fields of emerald barley and golden mustard. Scattered hamlets of stone and white-plaster houses, their flat roofs aflutter with bright prayer flags, dot the lower slopes on which yaks meander like vagrant shaggy boulders. Encircling hills, the colour of silence, hold aloft an aquamarine immensity of sky. Suddenly, my twenty-three-year-old guide, Tenzin, points to a distant sandy pass. 'There,' he says in Hindustani, 'that's the route His Holiness took when he escaped to India disguised as a soldier.' By a trick of the light in the high, thin air, the after-image of that historic exodus thirty-five years ago seems to hover on the horizon, giving meaning to a waiting landscape.

Tenzin's father, Tashi Tsering, was the Dalai Lama's personal chauffeur and accompanied the entourage that followed his master into exile to seek sanctuary in India from the Chinese crackdown in 1959. Tenzin, the youngest of eight children, was born in Dharamsala and returned to Tibet a year ago to work for a local tour agency. Our driver, Wangde, was born and brought up in Chinese-ruled Tibet and cannot read or write Tibetan, which was removed from the curricula of local schools and has been restored only recently. To show his solidarity with the Indo-Tibetan connection, Wangde shuts off the Chinese pop music on the stereo and puts on a Hindi film song. We roll into Lhasa to the tune of *Choli ke peechhe kya hai.*

Early next morning we set out on the 196-km journey to Zsetang, a small town in the Yarlung Zango (Brahmaputra) valley, which is considered to be the cradle of Tibetan civilization. The road to Zsetang is being built, and we bump and lurch over terrain which is more dirt than track. En route we stop to visit Samye monastery, built in the eighth century by Padmasambhava, the tantric sage from India, revered in Tibet as Guru Rimpoche. Zigzagging between sandbars, it takes two hours to cross the broad, shallow river in a wooden-hulled ferry. Mini tractors on the far side carry us to the monastery, bouncing over sand dunes. Like most other monasteries in Tibet, Samye was vandalized before and during the Cultural Revolution. Chapels were gutted and used to store grain; age-old frescoes were defaced with Maoist slogans; priceless images were smelted down into gold ingots or copper bullets. However, for his safety rather than mine, I don't question Tenzin too much about such matters. Even in today's tourist-friendly Tibet, walls have ears; a Tibetan friend of Tenzin's, who spoke too candidly to a foreign tour group, 'disappeared' four years ago and has never been heard of since. There are many thousands of similar cases. Their unknown fate underscores the fact that Tibet, real Tibet, reveals itself through absence, rather than what is present, a land which is what it is not, and is not what it is.

In Samye, as in many other places, restoration work is in progress. Only too late those whom the Tibetans call the 'occupiers' have realized that Buddhism is not merely the soul of Tibet but, more importantly, its most lucrative investment in terms of good public relation and tourist revenue. In the past few years, tourism has emerged not only as Tibet's potentially biggest foreign exchange earner but also as a source for generating more jobs for increasing numbers of Chinese migrants who will help in the ongoing process of the Sinoization of the country. As a Lhasa resident ironically remarked to me: 'As of today you are our most important export commodity.'

This ritual genuflection to local tradition shows through like the sham sincerity of a gold-toothed smile. In Samye, as in the Potala and other places of worship, the Chinese authorities are implementing 'sanitization' measures. The lambent glow of butter lamps is being superseded by the flat glare of electric lighting, purportedly to make the inscrutable face of Buddhism more accessible to foreign tourists. Many Tibetans, however, believe that the 'improvements' are designed to facilitate electronic surveillance of resident monks and visitors.

We reach Zsetang, the birthplace of Tibet. It was here that the patron deity of Tibet, Chenrezig—also known as the 1000-armed Avalokitesvara from whom the Dalai Lamas are incarnated—appeared in the avatar of a monkey who was to be the progenitor of the Tibetan race. Today, Zsetang's shabby main street is lined with Chinese noodle shops, hairdressing parlours and stalls selling plastic hats made in Tianjin. Seven kilometres away, on a rock hill, is the small dzong of Yongbulagong, built by the first king, Nyatri Tsanpo, and said to be the first building in Tibet. Destroyed during the Cultural Revolution, the dzong has been rebuilt and functions as a chapel attended by lay monks. The wizened caretaker gives me a vigorous thumbs-up sign on hearing that I am from India and asks for pictures of the Dalai Lama. I indicate, regretfully, that I have none; pictures of the Dalai Lama are prized in Tibet above even American cigarettes, those universal tokens of cross-cultural goodwill. On the altar, six large butter lamps burn; five are of silver and one is a tin bucket, subversive emblem of a dispossessed civilization.

In the evening we go to a local karaoke bar. Couples do a sedate foxtrot on the raw concrete floor, men with men and girls with girls, all in Western clothes. Like an electronic thangka, a large screen flickers with mesmeric images borrowed from Hong Kong MTV. The sing-along list has no Tibetan songs, and Tenzin and Wangde select their favourite

Chinese numbers which they belt out with gusto. I think of a tin bucket burning bright in the night over Yongbulagong.

It takes us ten hours to drive to Gyangtse, Tibet's fourth-largest town. We cross the 16,000-foot Kamba La pass with its spectacular views of the Nozin Khang glacier which looms over the brilliant blue of Yamdrok Tso, the aptly named Turquoise Lake. The vast lake has rich alluvial deposits of gold and a processing plant has been set up on its shore. Photography is prohibited and no vehicles are allowed to stop along this stretch. The lake is also said to contain gold of another sort; it is rumoured that some monasteries consigned their treasures to its deep water to prevent them from falling into the hands of looters. Yamdrok Tso conceals its secrets with an enigmatic blue that is reflected in the Buddha's eyes painted on a sentinel stupa.

Gyangtse's single dog-leg street is Chinese at one end, Tibetan at the other; tarred road and concrete abruptly give way to stone paving and ornately carved and painted window frames. Dominating both is the rocky outcrop crowned with the ruined fort destroyed by imperial artillery in 1904 when Younghusband led his historic expedition to open the Forbidden Kingdom to British trade. This feat-of-arms discouraged the growing Russian interest in the region, but inspired Manchu China to invade Kham in Eastern Tibet the following year. In 1910, the thirteenth Dalai Lama sought asylum in British India from the Chinese incursion and returned to Tibet in 1912 after the overthrow of the Manchu dynasty in the Chinese revolution of 1911.

On a well-paved road again, we drive to Shigatse, Tibet's second-largest town and totally Chinese in character. Shigatse's Tashilhunpo monastery, with its famous twenty-six-metre-high statue of the seated Maitreya (Future) Buddha, is the traditional seat of the Panchen Lama, whose office—created in the seventeenth century by the fifth Dalai Lama—has been exploited by successive Chinese regimes. The tenth and last Panchen Lama, born in 1938, spent most of his life in Chinese custody and died in suspicious circumstances in Shigatse in 1989. In 1992, an immense tomb, putatively plated with 700 kilograms of gold, was erected for him in Tashilhunpo, with the blessings of the Chinese authorities who picked up the bill.

Photography is prohibited in Tashilhunpo unless one pays a fifty-yuan fee per picture. Encouraged by the example of a group of Western tourists who are surreptitiously shooting away, I try to sneak a picture. The flash alerts three irate monks who descend on me, demanding I pay fifty yuan or have my film confiscated. I ask why others have been allowed to take photographs with impunity, while I, whose country has the honour to afford a haven to His Holiness, the Dalai Lama, am forced to pay. This seems to make matters worse. Sensing Tenzin's growing discomfiture, I finally agree to pay up, but insist on a receipt, in Tibetan, for the amount.

Later, I am told by a Tibetan: 'The people of Shigatse are very strange. They prefer the Chinese to the Tibetans. The monks will ask for pictures of Dalai Lama; if you give them any, they'll report you to the police.'

The next day, back in Lhasa, we visit the Potala, the labyrinthine heart of Tibet, filled now with an eloquent emptiness. Perched like a huge mythical bird with outspread wings atop Marpori, the Red Mountain, the Potala—derived from the Sanskrit Patolaka, the place where Avalokitesvara dwells—was built in the seventh century by King Songtsen Gampo during whose reign Buddhism was introduced into Tibet. The original structure was destroyed by lightning, and its reconstruction was taken up in the seventeenth century under the fifth Dalai Lama.

Completed after his death, the Potala—with over 1000 rooms housing 10,000 shrines and 200,000 images—became the winter residence of the Dalai Lamas. No nails were used to construct the wood and stone edifice, whose six-foot-thick outer walls were filled with molten copper to strengthen them against earthquakes.

During the 1959 uprising, the Potala, scene of some of the fiercest fighting, was shelled by the Chinese; it was saved from destruction by the reported intervention of Zhou Enlai. The building survived but only as a hollow husk, with the life force that sustained it having gone into exile.

This resonant emptiness rules the Potala today, magnified by the clatter of workmen installing electrical fittings which will banish forever the luminous shadows of faith. Of the 500 monks who lived and worshipped and worked in the Potala, only twenty-eight remain; the rest have gone, into hiding or prison. A group of Chinese, led by a Chinese-speaking guide, stop in front of a tapestry depicting Tsong Khapa, founder of the Gelupka sect, the so-called Yellow Hat order from which the Dalai Lamas have descended. Poker-faced, Tenzin interprets for me: 'He is saying that Tsong Khapa is the big Party boss, surrounded by his loyal Party workers.' The Chinese visitors nod approvingly at the karmic wheel of mythology reinvented.

In a tapestry-draped prayer room, used by the eighth to the fourteenth Dalai Lamas, an elderly monk identifies me as an Indian. He waits for the other tourists to file out and then invites me quickly to shoot as many pictures as I want, without paying a fee. 'It is just as well that China took Tibet,' he tells me through Tenzin. 'Otherwise maybe India would have gone. And then where would he be today, where would we all be?' He bows towards the vacant throne on which a single scarf is folded in silent expectation of a once and future presence.

In the afternoon we go to the Norbulinka, the summer residence of the Dalai Lama. Set in shady parkland, the Norbulinka complex was conceived by the seventh Dalai Lama in the mid-eighteenth century. The new Palace was built by the present Dalai Lama in 1954 and was badly damaged in 1959 and later by the depredations of the Cultural Revolution. The visit includes a tour of the restored living quarters, spartanly simple and containing homely icons of worship: a Philips radiogram bearing the emblem of the Ashoka pillar, a gift from India; a washbasin made by Shanks of Great Britain, now filled with grain and other votive offerings left by local visitors.

In a timber yard behind the Palace we discover the remains of two Baby Austins and a 1931 Dodge gifted to the thirteenth Dalai Lama. Carried piecemeal on yaks into Tibet where they were reassembled, these were the only three cars in the country. Disused after the thirteenth Dalai Lama's death, the cars were recommissioned in the 1950s by the present Dalai

Lama, Tenzin Gyatso, after whom, I suddenly realize, my guide is probably named.

The Baby Austins have rusted into scrap metal. The orange-coloured Dodge is half buried under a pile of junk—tyres gone, engine missing, but still recognizable as a vehicle. Tenzin places his hands reverentially on the broken body. 'My father used to drive this car,' he says. 'Do you think it could be made to work again ... if all the pieces were put back together?' His arms lift up as if to encompass the yard, the Norbulinka, Lhasa, the endless vacant sweep of land beyond. 'If it were all put together again?' he asks.

Doma Choden is trying to get the pieces together in her own way. Reading the signs of the times, Doma's father took his family out of Tibet three years before the 1959 uprising. Doma and her brother, Kesang, were educated in India, and later in the US. In the late 1980s, Kesang, an anthropologist, returned to Tibet to work in the villages, to trace traditional crafts and folkways which had been almost wiped out under Chinese rule. In 1990, Doma, with an Arts degree from Columbia University, joined him to help set up a joint sector carpet factory on the outskirts of Lhasa. The Khawachen Carpet and Wool Handicraft Company officially opened its doors on 6 June 1994.

In a large, well-lit hall, rows of women sit in front of handlooms, the clack of the wooden frames punctuating the strands of song they weave into the emerging pattern. The factory, which eventually hopes to have 300–500 people working and living on the premises, is a training centre as much as an export-oriented enterprise. 'During the Cultural Revolution, anyone who had any style, who wanted to paint a picture, make or wear jewellery, was denounced as a class enemy,' says Doma, and adds, quoting Vaclav Havel, 'Bad style encourages bad government.'

As she leans over a loom to study an intricate motif taking shape, it is clear that the design of living that Khawachen is seeking to fashion involves much more than just carpets. But it will take a loom subtler than any devised to re-weave a fabric whose one defining thread remains a singular absence.

You're No Great Sheikhs, Charlie Brown

We spent the Christmas of 1993 in Dubai as guests of our friends John and Anjoo Mason. It turned out to be a white Christmas. No, of course it never snows in Dubai. It was a white Christmas for Bunny and me because of our clenched-knuckle apprehension that, unwittingly, we might end up doing something that would embarrass our host and hostess, and in the process get ourselves deported from Dubai.

For the cardinal rule in Dubai is DRTB: Don't rock the boat. Inept landlubber that I am, rocking boats is one of my specialties. But for once I succeeded in leaving the boat unrocked. I didn't even ask why so many people one saw were wearing bed sheets in public.

There are no individual addresses in the UAE; if you want to receive mail you have to get a PO Box number. Complications are created when you entertain at your unnumbered home. 'Get to the Spinneys supermarket in Deira, turn left at the green mosque with the three minarets and straight on till you see the Reels and Threads boutique, turn right and our villa is the third on the left with the blue shutters,' instructs the host on the phone, and then sends his car and driver on a recce patrol of the locality to spot lost-looking people.

This lack of specific location sums up the plush life and uncertain times of the subcontinental white-collar expat in the Emirates. You are there all right, in the land of petrol and money: ensconced in your central A/C apartment complex in Abu Dhabi which seems like a hybrid of upscale Bombay and downscale Miami Beach, or your split-level villa in Jumeirah where the neo-Disneyland architecture imparts the same startled look to the sunlight that it has in the exurban wilds of Southern California. But where exactly is there; and, more importantly, for how long?

The golden bubble which cocoons the expat can suddenly burst, for any real or surmised trespass: resident visa khallas; take the next plane home. 'After this Ayodhya business, some Pakistanis and Indian Muslims staged a demonstration. Apparently, a few stones were thrown at a Hindu temple in Bur-Dubai and at a couple of school buses. The next day, 14,000 people were deported. Pakistan protested. The home minister here came on TV and said only a "handful" had been expelled. Some hand! Of course the local papers didn't mention a word about any of it,' confided an expat.

Like everyone else, newspapers too must mind their ps and qs. The editor of a local daily had his passport taken into custody by the authorities four months ago when his paper published a sheikh's name in the wrong news story. 'It was a computer error, totally inoffensive. And the paper printed an apology the next day,' said one journalist. 'But the editor had his passport taken away "pending further investigation". And mind, it wasn't even one of the big sheikhs, just a sidey one. You've got to be really careful here.' In another incident, the editor of a weekend magazine reportedly lost her job because of an outspoken article she wrote on Kashmir.

'What nonsense!' snorts a dissenter. 'This isn't Saudi where two Filipino Christians were sentenced to be executed on Christmas Day for proselytizing. This is a progressive country—God's own economic haven, the world's answer to post-1997 Hong Kong. No personal income tax. Practically no inflation. Free trading in any currency you want. Dash it, they even let you drink, even in public, if you have a permit. Women don't have to be in purdah and can go out and work if they want. You have freedom of worship. Just don't make a public display of your religious or political beliefs. Work, make money, enjoy a good life. Just remember the official policy—DRTB. Don't rock the boat!'

The trouble is that one is never quite sure which is the boat one is not meant to rock. The result is that one is constantly double-guessing, adding two and two and getting Catch-22. On our first day in the UAE, I talked Bunny out of wearing her Snoopy and Charlie Brown T-shirt. The reason: Charles Shultz, the creator of Charlie Brown and Snoopy, has a Jewish-sounding name, which was printed on the T-shirt. Marks and Spencer products are banned in the UAE, because of the Jewish connection, as is Chivas Regal whisky for the same reason. Chivas is available only in Fujairah, an oil-poor emirate where the sheikhs are said to resort to dubious trade practices like dealing in fake visas in order to make a few extra dirhams.

As it is, I needn't have worried about Snoopy and Charlie Brown: Shultz's comic strip is daily featured in the *Khaleej Times*. An expat, however, still shudders at the memory of having unwittingly smuggled into the country a copy of Dr Seuss' children's classic *Green Eggs And Ham*. 'Had I been nabbed, it would have been khallas for me,' he said. All references to pigs and pork products are scrupulously edited out of children's textbooks. Yet, curiously enough, pork products are freely, though discreetly, available in supermarkets like Spinneys and Lamcy, behind a counter that says 'Not for Muslims'.

But though pork might selectively be kosher, messy paan remains totally taboo in a spanking clean, hygiene-conscious environment that could make Switzerland look slovenly in comparison. 'To get my paans I have to go to a black-market dealer in Bur-Dubai, as though I'm buying illicit sharab,' moaned Sakina, a housemaid from eastern UP. 'The shame of it!'

On a more spiritual level, a section of the local Bengali community is said to have smuggled in a couple of genuine Kumartulli images for Durga Puja. 'Getting them in was not too tough, but immersion was a real problem,' said an expat.

'Finally someone took them out in a motorboat at night and dumped them in the Arabian Gulf.'

Hassles regarding paans and *protima*s notwithstanding, most subcontinentals—not excluding the contractual labourers who are herded into camps and taken in cattle trucks to and from the construction sites where they work—feel they have a better life than they could aspire to at home. 'The social pecking order is clearly demarcated,' said an expat. 'Right on top are the sheikhs, who are not above the law but, simply, are the law. Then come the British and American expats whom everyone toadies up to, including most of the locals. After that you have Arabs from elsewhere, like the Syrians or Kuwaitis or the Palestinians, whom everyone despises, but not openly. And right at the bottom you have what they call the SCNs, subcontinental nationals: Indians, Pakistanis, Bangladeshis, and—for some strange reason—Filipinos as well.'

Despite their relatively lowly status, Indians play an increasingly significant role in various fields, including journalism, advertising, and education. Starting with twenty-two pupils in 1968, the Varkey group, of Indian origin, today comprises a network of twelve schools with a total of 22,000 students. According to one estimate, 65 per cent of Dubai's municipal transport is operated by Indians. Half the shops in the famous gold souk, where the yellow metal hangs like meat in a butcher's shop to be sold by the kilo, are run by Gujaratis. 'If they threw the Indians out, they'd have to shut down the economy,' said an SCN with a confidence which sounds a little too hearty to be true.

For many Indians, the Emirates represent the last—and best—hope of a good life, an ideal blend of East and West where Hindustani is widely understood, domestic servants are available, the civic amenities are unimpeachable, and the supermarkets are stocked with both familiar and exotic goodies, all at practically throwaway prices.

'The thing to do is make your whack in three years, then take the full benefit of the TR (transfer of residence) rules and go back home with your American car, microwave, freezer, and what have you,' says a Sharjah Indian. Housewives scan the supermarket ads, rush to the store offering a discount on a bag of potato chips, and at the end of the month go to the gold souk to buy another addition to the nest egg the family is squirrelling away for the inevitable day of return to India.

For those who care to take time off from the dedicated pursuit of money, the Emirates offer an unexpected range of recreational activities: unspoilt beaches, verdant golf courses, water sports, exploring the desert in dune buggies, and 'wadi-bashing'—trekking the dried-up riverbeds of the wadis through a surrealist rockscape dreamt up by Salvador Dali.

But outdoors or indoors, everyone keeps a weather eye open for the slightest change in the climate, cultural or meteorological. 'Up until a couple of years ago you couldn't have any Christmas or New Year festivities openly. But this year we not only had a programme of carol singing on local TV but also an Egyptian belly dance at a private party in the Dubai International Hotel. I wonder what it signifies,' muses an expat.

The changing social scene is matched by environmental metamorphosis. In a land where bottled water is more expensive than petrol, the ultimate status symbol is greenery, cultivated at astronomical cost. Palm-fringed Abu Dhabi looks as lush as Florida, and flower-bordered Al Ain is more of a garden city than Bangalore. The progressive greening of the desert has had unexpected side effects.

'The mausam is certainly changing,' confirmed Amiruddin, a driver from Tamil Nadu who came to Dubai five years ago after paying Rs 20,000 for sponsorship to an agent in India. 'Last year there was a big storm here. There was thunder and lightning and the streets all got flooded. The locals hadn't ever seen anything like it and many wailed and prayed, fearing the wrath of Allah had descended on them for letting in all these foreign influences.'

It's enough to make Charlie Brown mutter 'Good grief!' in apprehension.

Where Hanuman Is
Worshipped in French

Bunny and I reached Mauritius in May 1992. A week after my colleague Bachi Karkaria had left it. The Mauritian Tourism Board was quite sniffy about it. She's just left, and you've turned up, said MTB. What are you two going to find to write about without repeating each other?

Don't worry, I said. We'll find something. And we did. I didn't recognize Bachi's Mauritius, and I don't think she did mine. It's not just that Bachi and I are different. It's that Mauritius is so different from anything else. Including itself.

On my first day in Mauritius, my local guide, Mooniar, asked me a riddle as we were finishing lunch. 'The British stir the sugar into their tea this way,' he said, stirring clockwise. 'The French stir it this way,' he continued, going anticlockwise. 'But we Mauritians stir it this way,' he said, describing a zigzag in his cup. 'Why? No? Give up?' I conceded defeat. 'To make it tasty!' beamed Mooniar, delighted by his own punchline.

It's a good line to remember, and apt for the tiny island in the Indian Ocean, 850 kilometres off the coast of Madagascar, which has been stirred by the zigzag cross-currents of history so as to impart to it its unique savour. The visitor gets a taste of this special flavour soon after arrival at the Sir Seewoosagar Ramgoolam International Airport in Plaisance. Driving through the morning streets you see roadside kiosks selling an intriguing combination of baguettes and pakoras. The shop signs present an equally unusual cultural mélange: mostly French or English, with a sprinkling of Chinese interspersed with the Hindu symbol 'Om'.

In the countryside, the vegetation is as variegated as the hoardings. The silk-smooth highway, comparable with roads in Western Europe, unspools through a gently rolling landscape cloaked with feathery sugar cane fields like the green wings of a giant bird outspread across the land. At times you feel you could be driving through Normandy, with cane plantations having replaced pastures. A bend in the road—and you are engulfed in lush tropical vegetation. A crest, and suddenly between two jagged volcanic peaks on the horizon, the Indian Ocean greets you with a wink of startling, aquamarine blue.

Set in the sea like a grain of the sugar which continues to be the mainstay of its economy, Mauritius has been like a tea cup in the stormy tides of change. The Dutch, who came in 1598, were the first settlers, naming Mauritius after Maurice of Nassau. They cut down the ebony forests, introduced sugar cane, brought in Malagasy slaves, and drove the dodo into extinction. The Dutch abandoned the island in 1710, and were replaced by the French. Following the Napoleonic wars, the British took over Mauritius, abolished slavery, and imported indentured Indian labour to work the cane plantations. Mauritius gained independence in 1968 and in 1979 embarked on an ambitious programme of industrial and commercial development. Today, Mauritius is a republic and is set to prove its credentials as Africa's first economic tiger. A lot of change to be crammed into so small an island, measuring only 1865 square kilometres in area and with a population of little over a million.

The visitor often feels that he is watching a cavalcade of tableaux from three continents parading past in the blink of an eye. This dance to the rhythm of time finds an apt expression in the Sega, the Mauritian version of folk disco. The Sega traces its origins to the era of slavery, when plantation workers would gather in the evening to recreate in song and dance half-remembered memories of their lost African homeland. Today, the Sega—an ebullient admixture of calypso, Moorish flamenco, and Polynesian hula—is a tourist attraction. Sega bands perform in the five-star beach hotels, the Creole dancers in their swirling skirts coaxing guests to join in the hip-sprung, up-tempo beat. Few of the participating visitors realize that what they are celebrating is, in effect, a liberation from chains.

For those who want to experience it, there is a constant sense of a double vision which lends an added dimension to the picture-postcard image of a tourist paradise—which indeed Mauritius is. The silver beaches, the crystal-clear blue lagoons, 'smooth as a baby's bath' as a travel brochure enthuses, the verdant hillsides, and the whispering groves of palm trees compose an ideal getaway for the holidaymaker. Deluxe hotels like the Sofitel Imperial at Wolmar and the Maritim at Balaclava offer luxurious accommodation and a gourmet selection of Continental cuisine and indigenous Creole fare, tinged with the smoky taste of Africa. Visitors can chance their luck at one of the several casinos on the island, shop for a variety of duty-free bargains, including gold and precious gems, or try their hand at water sports like wind surfing, snorkelling, and deep-sea fishing.

But for those willing to make the translation from tourist to traveller, there is another Mauritius beyond the glossy wrapping of a package holiday. In its own way, this other Mauritius is equally imbued with fantasy, a landscape of imaginary homelands revealed through random encounters which the visitor takes back in the form of mental snapshots. My own collection of Mauritian close-ups includes the face of Ram Gopal, a fifty-five-year-old man in search of his own history.

I met Ram Gopal on the public beach at Flic-en-Flac, at the edge of a casuarina grove strewn with Sunday picnickers. Ram was selling batik scarves and dodo T-shirts. I indicated I wasn't a customer. 'You from India?' he asked, the unfamiliar English Gallicized. I said I was, and Ram Gopal introduced himself. Switching to rusty Hindustani, he told me that his dada's dada, grandfather's grandfather, Gopal, had been brought to Mauritius from Bihar. Unable to pronounce his surname, the British had appended a number to his first name, which his descendants had adopted as the family name.

Ram had been to Bihar once, years ago, but had been unable to trace his ancestral village, or his family, whose name he did not know. Bihar was so big; there had been so many Gopals.

Ram was keen on establishing a business link with India, exporting scarves and shirts. He had met a visitor from Bombay, who had said he owned a shop and would do a partnership dhandha with Ram. He had taken a thousand rupees worth of goods, on credit. Ram had never heard from him again.

Was I interested in doing dhandha? I explained I wasn't a businessman, didn't have a shop. Perhaps I knew someone who did have a shop, would do business with Ram? Anyway, even if I didn't, here was Ram's identity card, I could take down the details. Did I have an official card? I gave him my business card. He nodded, acknowledging the mutual affirmation of identity, and walked away.

Establishing identities is not always easy in Mauritius. When I asked Mooniar if he was of Indian extraction, he said no, he was Tamil. A Hindu? No. Did he go to a mosque then? No, no, hadn't he said he was Tamil? He went to a temple of course. To Mooniar, Hindus were Hindi-speaking people who had come from Bihar.

The language of religion affords many ambiguities in Mauritius. Visiting Ganga Talav, to which thousands of Hindu devotees flock on the night of Mahashivaratri, I climbed the hill to the statue of Hanuman, presented by Atal Behari Vajpayee when he was India's external affairs minister during the Janata regime. A Mauritian family was offering prayers to the image. The Hindu revivalist leader's visions of Akhand Bharat would have gained a new perspective to hear Hanuman being worshipped in chaste French.

On my last night in Mauritius I went down to the bar of the Sand 'N' Dory to have a farewell beer with Mario, the Creole barman. Mario said he had wanted to marry a Hindu girl called Premila. Premila's parents had objected, because he was a Creole, and had sent Premila to India, where she had never been before. Mario began to sing softly. He stopped and took a sip of beer. That was Premila's favourite song, he said. She had taught him to sing it. But he couldn't understand Indian. Would I tell him what the song meant? He began to sing again, slowly, waiting for me to translate.

Janay woh kaise, log thay jinke, pyar ko pyar mila
Humne to jab kaliyan mangi, kaanto ka haar mila

(Who knows who they were, whose love was returned with love
When I asked for flowers I got a garland of thorns)

Stir it which way you like, Mauritius has an unforgettable flavour.

Twiga, the Last Giraffe

We went on a Kenyan safari in 1997. On a similar expedition in the 1950s (though he used a rifle, rather than a camera) Hemingway wrote The Green Hills of Africa. *I'm no Hemingway. And I wondered who would describe for me the breathtaking beauty of Africa. Fortunately, Twiga was there to oblige.*

Jambo! which is how we say namaste in Africa. I'm Twiga, the giraffe, welcoming you to my home in Masai Mara, the Kenyan part of the famous Serengeti sanctuary, the largest wildlife sanctuary in the world.

Masai Mara is the home of the so-called Big Five of Africa: Tembo, the elephant; Kifaru, the double-horned rhinoceros; Simba, the lion king; the buffalo; and the leopard. But for all the top billing the Big Five get, in all modesty I must confess that I'm really the star of the show. With my long, graceful neck, sinuous walk and curving eyelashes, I've often been compared to a Vogue model, whoever or whatever that might be. Parading the high savannah, I'm the elegant, italicized signature scripted across the page of Africa.

My home, Masai Mara, is beautiful. A sweep of gently undulating grassland, dotted with the flat-topped, anvil-shaped acacia trees on which the golden hammer of the sun arcs down from a sky of thunderbolt blue. Once this endless sea of grass teemed with surging tides of life—sharp-horned eland and dancing gazelle; snorting warthog and striped pyjama-suited zebra; majestically ambling elephant and that comically ferocious-looking chap called the wildebeest. The great herds of old have all gone now, leaving just a few of us survivors. But as though to fill the gap, a new breed of creature called the tourist has appeared on the scene. Uh-oh, here come two of them now. I suppose I'd better get ready to have my picture taken, for the umpteenth time today.

One of the creatures is a sorry-looking specimen with a long, beaky nose, unruly mop of white-grey hair, and pouches under the eyes. The other is far prettier and perkier, with bright, intelligent eyes and an engaging smile. From what I can gather, they are named respectively, the Jug and the Bunny. I've been told that the Jugs and the Bunnys of humankind represent the two genders, but I have a sneaky suspicion that they actually constitute two totally different species, with the Bunnys being by far the superior of the two. For instance, look what's happening right now.

Paul, the driver-guide of the eight-seater motor van with the raisable roof in which the Jug and the Bunny are travelling, has stopped ten feet from where I'm patiently posing to have my picture taken, politely stifling a yawn of boredom. I'm getting a crick in my neck, waiting and wondering how long it can possibly take anyone, even a Jug, to fire off a quick snapshot and get it over with. In the meantime, the Jug is furiously struggling with the shutter button of the camera, cussing and swearing a blue streak about German products and how they should have got a Japanese one instead which would 'effing' well work when you 'effing' well wanted it to. I'm tempted to point out to him that the 'effing' thing, as he calls it, would have an 'effing' chance to work if only he would remember to open the 'effing' lens cover first, which he hasn't. But we've been told strictly not to communicate with humans, and we wildlife believe in following rules— which is more than can be said of humans, particularly the Jugs. Fortunately for all concerned, the Bunny finally takes the camera away from the Jug, opens the lens cover and takes my picture. As we say here, Hakuna matata—no problem. To reward her, I give her my best three-quarter profile, fluttering eyelashes and all.

Just then, a vanload of excited Koreans screeches to a stop in a cloud of dust. As I turn to do my number for them, Paul drives the Jug and the Bunny away to where his keen eyes have spotted a pair of magnificent black-maned lions snoozing in the shade of a bush, bellies distended with a lunch of freshly killed buffalo, totally oblivious to the chattering, camera-clicking ring of vehicles surrounding them.

Like most of the 800,000 other tourists who will visit Kenya this year, the Jug and the Bunny are on a safari. Ably organized by a Nairobi-based outfit called Across Africa, and booked through Narula Travels, Delhi, the six-night, seven-day package which includes four-star accommodation, sumptuous meals, overland transport, and the services of a guide-cum-driver is a snip at 1000 US dollars a head. The safari takes in Amboseli National Park, where the elephants roam like a slow-motion avalanche of great boulders under the sentinel snows of Mount Kilimanjaro; the shimmering expanse of Lake Nakuru over which pink clouds of flamingos rise, exhalations of a sleeping giant dreaming of candy floss; the exquisitely manicured lawns of the exclusive Mount Kenya Safari Club, once the stately home of Hollywood movie star William Holden and now said to be part-owned by arms dealer Adnan Khashoggi (and they call us wildlife); and lastly, an enormous feast of roast meat at the appropriately named Carnivore restaurant in Nairobi, where guests are force-fed till they signify surrender by laying flat a small white flag placed on their table.

During all of this the Jug and the Bunny display their very different traits. The Jug is pigheaded, pompous, irascible, insensitive, and generally inept, though not actually ill-intentioned. The Bunny on the contrary is accommodating, communicative, cheerful, and quick to tune in to the nuances and rhythms of local idioms and custom, swapping Asanti (Thank you) and Karibu (You're welcome) with the aplomb of a seasoned Africa hand. Little wonder then that everyone from hotel waiters to tour guides happily hastens to ask if they can do anything for the Bunny, while giving the Jug a wide berth, indicating with an apprehensive sideways nod and a rolling of eyeballs: What about *him*?

The difference is nowhere more manifest than when they visit a village of the Masai, the statuesquely tall tribe of cattle herders who live on a diet of cow's milk and blood mixed together. While the Bunny quickly establishes a sign-language sorority with the Masai women, probably exchanging milkshake recipes, the Jug haggles with the menfolk over the price of a knobkerrie, the traditional wooden war club. The transaction evokes the twin male characteristics of acquisitiveness and aggression, two sides of the same coin which sums up the unedifying story of mankind.

Fortunately, there are increasing signs that the Bunny-ness, so to speak, of humankind is asserting itself to redress the grievous imbalance caused by the Jug-ness of history which has not only despoiled so much of my beautiful home of Masai Mara but also endangered that far larger home of all of us, this battered and bloodied planet on which soon there may only be an empty desolation to mark the spot where once walked Twiga, the last giraffe. And the tourists are left to take pictures of each other, in the absence of anything else.

Why Is Red Square Closed?

We visited Russia in late 1993, after the dissolution of the USSR. The commissar may officially have been banished, but the thought-police still lurked in the shadows of the mind.

It wasn't just Red Square that was closed and inaccessible. So was most information, in a society still regimented by the need-not-to-know principle.

How do you distinguish between a loaf of bread and a telephone directory in Moscow? The answer to the riddle is both simple and significant: There is a long queue for the bread, but none for the directory. People queue for bread because there is a chance that when you get to the head of the line there will be a loaf still left. No one queues for a directory for the good and valid reason that the very few directories that do exist are kept securely under lock and key by their possessors and are not to be had for love or debased money on the public distribution system. This simple fact is symptomatic of a situation of acute scarcity in which the most scarce commodity is information itself, the most basic and important of all commodities. The paucity of directories reflects what might be called the need-not-to-know principle, an obdurate hangover from the spirit of the pre-glasnost era which has not been exorcized but merely reincarnated in the masquerade of a market economy.

The need-not-to-know formula is based on a line of logic as formidably unassailable as the Stalinist architecture which characterizes Russia's capital city: If you have a legitimate reason to phone someone, you must obviously know the person well enough to have his telephone number, in which case you do not need a directory; if you do not have his number, you just as obviously have no business to want to call him, in which case again a directory is unnecessary.

The visitor is confronted by the need-not-to-know factor even before he reaches Russia. His visa is stamped not on his passport but on a separate sheet which is detached on his departure, leaving no record on his documents as to whether he ever went to Russia at all. This breeds a sense of one's own unreality vis-à-vis one's location, an unease compounded by the gigantism of Stalin's Moscow which, seemingly, was designed to reduce the individual to an insignificant cipher which no one need ever know about, least of all the individual himself. The 6000-bed Rossiya seems less a mega hotel than a monstrous repository for dead souls left over from Gogol. Vast thoroughfares like Kutuzovsky Prospect appear to be built to accommodate the juggernaut roll of tanks or the landing of great air carriers rather than to cater to everyday traffic, leave alone the sightseeing pedestrian—that most inquisitive and difficult to monitor of all subversive elements.

The best way to get around Moscow is by its justly acclaimed underground Metro system. Visitors, however, face two small problems, again based on the need-not-to-know principle: All the station signs are in Russian, and even if one manages to read the Cyrillic script there are no readily accessible route maps to tell one where to make the required connections to reach one's destination. In the days when the Metro was built, it was presumed that either you knew where you were going and how, in which case you didn't need a map, or you didn't know, in which case you shouldn't have a map in the first place. Now touts hang around outside Metro stations, selling route maps to out-of-towners at 4000 roubles (approximately thirty paise). Not only is the print on these maps so small as to require the use of a magnifying glass (and where do you find a map which tells you where to get that?) but also, to confuse the issue further, the names of many stations have been changed to rid them of their communist associations.

Fortunately, I had with me my Swiss army knife with its built-in magnifying lens, and Bunny's facility with languages enabled us to crack the Cyrillic code within thirty-six hours of our arrival in the city. With her help I soon realized that in Russian PECTOPAH equals RESTORAN (P=R, E=E, C=S, T=T, etc), admittedly a slender semantic key with which to try and open the lock of Moscow's enigma.

For though the *New York Times* now publishes an edition in Russian, in terms of the communication of practical information Moscow remains a closed book. The almost total lack of signage renders the cityscape into an architectural alphabet unrelated to a comprehensible language. This can give rise to a need-not-to-go situation, as experienced by tourists who, unable to find a public convenience while visiting the exhibition grounds extolling the erstwhile USSR's industrial and agricultural achievements, must eventually make known to bemused locals their urgent need to go by resorting to nursery pantomime.

Anxious not to undergo a performance of this commonplace scenario, I initially enlisted the services of Yuri, a sixty-four-year-old non-English-speaking Russian who drove an eight-year-old Lada comparatively almost as well-preserved as himself. For thirty US dollars a day, Yuri was to be our friendly driver, philosopher, and guide in Moscow. Riding shotgun with him was Palina, an eighteen-year-old English-speaking university student who was to act as translator. But translation can prove a tricky business when undertaken within the need-not-to-know context, as we were to discover.

The first stop on our itinerary was Red Square. As we approached, there was a sudden clatter of steel-shod boots on cobblestones as uniformed militiamen cordoned off the area. What's happening? I asked. Red Square is closed, replied Palina. Ask them why, I said, indicating the uniforms. She looked at me blankly. You never, ever, asked uniforms anything; they asked you. In the absence of information, conjecture floated in the frosty air like wisps of vapour. Someone had kidnapped Lenin's embalmed body, displayed in the crypt outside the Kremlin. The militia had gone on strike. There had been a coup.

Then, as suddenly as they had appeared, the uniforms disappeared. Red Square is now open, declared Palina. We ventured out onto the frozen sea of black stone. At the far end, the brightly painted domes of St Basil's Cathedral huddled together like gossiping turbans. The bluff facade of the GUM shopping arcade faced the turreted walls of the Kremlin, stillborn capitalism confronting outworn socialism. In between, the vast vista seemed hemmed in by a horizon of uncertainty. Red Square had been closed. Then it had been opened. Would it be closed again, trapping us inside?

Yuri took us to a Finnish department store, sleek shelves crammed with Dutch cheeses, American cigarettes, and Swiss chocolates. At the cash desk they demanded dollars. I want Ruski products for Ruski roubles, I insisted. Yuri and Palina confabulated. Ruski things not good for you, said Palina. You buy here. For a packet of cold meats, a crusty loaf, cheese, and the cheapest bottle of wine I could find, I paid 18 dollars 75 cents, almost equivalent to a Russian schoolteacher's salary for a month. But Yuri and Palina looked approving. Why? I did not need to know.

We drove out to Zagorsk, forty kilometres from Moscow. The road sped past birch forests aflame with autumn colours, dachas with gaily painted eaves peering demurely out like matrushka dolls. We explored the walled monastery complex, its sombre churches incongruously topped with bright blue and gold domes.

Outside, I spotted a bar selling pivo, Russian beer. Pivo, I said, pointing. No, said Palina firmly. Not good. Please to get in auto. By now I knew better than to ask why. Yuri took us to a place which welcomed American Express in three languages and where the cheapest soup was seven dollars. I ordered a large Stolichnaya vodka, the only genuinely Russian item on the menu.

Determined to try and see the real Moscow, the next day we dumped Yuri and Palina. Mentally reciting the mnemonic mantra PECTOPAH=RESTORAN we braved the Metro. And all at once the closed and daunting city seemed to open for us. We took the train to Arbat and strolled along the pedestrian precinct, past street-side painters and musicians and the house where Pushkin had lived; looked at the queues for McDonald's hamburgers, ate local ice-cream cones tasting of cardboard, and joined the throngs in GUM shopping for Italian fashions and Indian Lakme cosmetics; walked past the Lubyanka and down Gorky Street, buying a crisp baguette from a hawker for sixty roubles, and took the train back to Krylatskoye in the high-rise suburb where our guest flat was situated.

We emerged from the station. Under a hoarding heralding the 31 flavours of Baskin and Robbins, a street market was in progress: a jumble of beets, turnips, second-hand canvas shoes, rusty farming tools. In the cold drizzle, a woman sat hunched by herself, ancient, immobile as the earth in which her swollen legs seemed rooted. In front of her, on a scrap of newspaper, was a single sprig of parsley, votive offering to a fugitive deity.

How long had she been there in the cold and wet, how long would she remain, what infinitesimal hope of profit could she glean from that solitary stalk of wilted leaves? I did not know. Nor, at last I realized, should I need to know, not in this new Moscow whose faceless tower blocks reared around us, monoliths standing sentinel over their own anonymity which acknowledged no past nor conceded any future.

Kafka, Cedok, and the Mystic Pizza

Bunny and I got to Czechoslovakia in 1991 shortly after Marxism had given way to market forces. In Prague, under the shadow of Kafka's castle, the Chicago Express Pizza had opened shop.

I wondered what Kafka would have made of it all. Would he have written an allegory about a man who woke up one day to discover that overnight he had metamorphosed into a giant thick crust with extra cheese topping? And what would K have made of Cedok, whose unseen presence seemed to shadow my footsteps?

An editor of the *Times of India* once told me that in a former corporate avatar he had, Diogenes-like, lived for five days in a beer barrel in Prague. Discretion precluded my asking if the barrel, or the future editor, had been full or empty during the sojourn, and in what proportion. But the thought of beer barrels doing double duty as temporary accommodation kept haunting me as I planned my own trip to Czechoslovakia.

The third secretary, press and information, in the Czech embassy in New Delhi hadn't heard about beer barrels. But he had heard of Prague hotels at US $180 per pax per night. I said I would stick with the barrels. The guide book was vague both about barrels and hotels: 'Arrive early and get in line at one of the two room-finding services,' it advised, adding ominously, '... the tension in these offices often stops just short of actual physical violence ...' I began to glean a new insight into Kafka's castle.

In London I went to Cedok, the official Czechoslovakian tourism agency. Budget accommodation, yes? Pliss fill and sign ze requisite requisition form, said the severely smiling young woman behind the desk. I partially filled and signed, leaving provisional our dates of arrival and departure, which had still to be confirmed. Goot, said the young woman, I haf just now made your booking. Give fifteen pounds, pliss. I said I did not have fifteen pounds to give right then, not to mention confirmed dates. The young woman's smile grew severer. Without fifteen pounds your booking is invalid, she said. I shall send you ze bill for ze booking. Zat is my last word. I was about to point out that for an invalid booking the bill must also be invalid. But the young woman gave me a smile of such dazzling severity that I slipped into my beer-barrel mode and left before she could stop just short of actual physical violence to her lip muscles.

In the London phone book I found 'Czechbook Agency: for private accommodation in Prague'. A Knightsbridge voice instructed me to remit the tariff and receive by return post the name and address of my host in Prague. Fingers crossed, I sent the money. Back came the name, Ing Josef Oliberius, with a Prague address and phone number. Thank God, no beer barrels, said Bunny. But I wasn't so sanguine.

True, in the twinkling of a magic lantern, the 'velvet revolution' had, like a conjurer's cloak, whisked away the iron fist of authoritarianism. I knew it. So, probably, did Vaclav Havel. But had anyone told Cedok? Spring had sprung again in Prague. Could a Cedok winter be far behind? Zat is my last word: the last words rang forebodingly in my mind.

In London, my sleep was troubled with dreams in which a pale, ascetic man in a garret wrote the predestined sentence of a trial yet to begin: 'Someone must have slandered Jug S, because one morning, without his having done anything wrong, he was arrested ...' The next morning, on the breakfast table was a communication from Cedok, a bill for. cancelled, unbooked accommodation. I shivered. Someone had walked over my beer barrel. Or Kafka's.

We landed at Prague airport at ten in the night. Bare concrete floor, unshaded light bulbs, a huddle of trench coats with collars turned up like spies come in from the cold. It looked like a set for a B-grade Hollywood version of a 1970s' John le Carre novel. The emigration officer glanced at our passports and pressed a buzzer summoning two men wreathed in cigarette smoke and rumpled suspicion. If this had been a movie script, one of them would have taken the cigarette stub out of his mouth and said: Your papers are not in order, pliss. One of them took the stub out of his mouth and said: Your papers are not in order, pliss. Come wiz us. Had Cedok struck?

But it wasn't Cedok. It was our Indian passports. Tourists from the subcontinent were required to deposit with their local Czech embassies a large sum of money as indemnity to guarantee their return home and/or carry with them a minimum of US $1000 each for their visit. We failed on both counts. The man sans stub tapped his chin with our passports: Karla confronting George Smiley across Checkpoint Charlie—turn him back, or let him in and give him enough rope to hang himself? All right, he said. The long rope had won. We went to Customs to find our luggage had been left in Paris. The mills of Cedok grind slowly...

Outside, Ing Oliberius waited for us, a big leather-jacketed man with an air of distracted jollity like the good soldier Schweik gone AWOL. Promising to rescue our luggage the next day, he bundled us into an old but serviceable Lada. We drove through deserted streets to a semi-detached house in a wooded, hilly suburb. Ing Oliberius ushered us into our self-contained 'granny flat': sitting room, bedroom, bathroom, kitchenette, black-and-white TV, no beer barrels—our home away from home for the next six days, safe from Cedok for the moment.

The following morning, we discovered that 'Ing' as in Oliberius stood for 'engineer', our host's profession. He had once worked on an engineering project in Lahore—close to India, no? No, we agreed, thinking of the convoluted geography of politics.

There were other home thoughts from abroad. Like India, Czechoslovakia is at a crossroads where liberalization intersects with a protected economy. We can go now all places in Europe, no visa, said Ing Oliberius. But only if we have this, he added, flicking a non-existent coin with his thumb. The devalued Czech currency is now pegged at about forty-four crowns to one pound sterling, almost the same as the Indian rupee. Devaluation has virtually done away with the once flourishing black market in foreign exchange. Increasing privatization has done away with a lot of jobs: there are half a million unemployed in a total population of fifteen million. Come the new year with its further promised reforms, and many more casualties are predicted, among them residents of government-subsidized housing complexes where rents are expected to double to 1200 crowns and above a month, a sizeable bite out of a middle-class salary of 3000 to 4000 crowns.

But to fill the void, the wintry sky above historic Wenceslas Square yielded an appropriate manna, with six exciting new toppings: World-famous Chicago Express Pizza was here. And Praguers thronged to sample a foretaste of capitalist logos made flesh, and ketchup and mozzarella cheese. Like the overnight ice on its cobblestones, the city that Kundera called a disappearing poem on a burning sheet of paper was recrystallizing in a reflection on a plate-glass window inscribed with a fast-food slogan. Above it loomed Prague castle, Kafka's citadel, its gothic spires like brooding eagles of the mind, hooded and jessed after flight.

Cutting through Stare Mesto, the old town, we crossed the Moldau River over Karlov Most, the city's oldest bridge, and followed winding streets that led like an argument of insidious intent to the Hradcany district and Prague castle. Within the castle walls is Golden Lane, a small street of tiny houses in one of which Kafka lived briefly. Trying to take a snapshot of the house, I ended up with a close-up of the backs of three Germanic heads. From yesterday's non-person, Kafka has become today's instant crowd-puller, like Chicago Express. On the way down I had a fleeting vision of a writer penning a midnight fable about a young man whose metamorphosis into a giant pizza is greeted by his family with initial revulsion, which turns into acceptance, and then into a franchise concession, in a latter-day replay of the miracle of the Eucharist.

Returning to Ing Oliberius's, we found our lost luggage waiting for us. A suitcase lock was broken, a pair of shoes missing. Cedok's eye for an eye, a pair of shoes for a bootless bill? A tame ending, even for mass-consumption Kafka.

But there is a postscript. Back in Delhi, a message from London: the missing shoes have been located. There is also another bill from Cedok, duly being forwarded to us. The game is still afoot; the shadow play continues. For while the vestigial shade of Cedok lingers, Joseph K, too, must await his final exorcism from the beer barrel of history.

Ode on a Grecian Turn

Most countries come in twos. There is the real country, where real-life people live and work and generally do their thing; and there's its touristy counterpart, where weirdly dressed people from foreign parts spend large amounts of time and money trying to discover the real country, which of course remains forever elusive to them.

Greece is different. For it comes not in two, but in three. The real Greece and two distinct tourist Greeces. The Historic Tour Greece, which is all about Culture with a capital 'C', and the Islands' Cruise, which is all about Pleasure, also upper-case.

I've forgotten most of the Culture I picked up. But those horrendous wine prices on board the cruise ship still haunt me.

Kali mera, ladies and gentlemen, which means good morning in Greek and is not to be confused with kalamari, which is fried squid, a Greek delicacy, which you will have opportunity to taste later on during this seven-day Best of Historic Greece tour. Yes? Gentleman in the back with big nose and nice lady has question? And the question is: When later? And the answer is later later. Food, even kalamari, is always later than culture on Historic Greece tour.

In seven days we will cover 1500 kilometres of mainland Greece, including the Peloponnese, and 3000 years of the history of Greece, cradle of western civilization which gave the world everything from the Olympic Games to the first atomic theory propounded by Democritus; from Aristotle the philosopher, third-century BC, to Aristotle the shipping tycoon, twentieth-century AD, better known as Mr Jacqueline

Kennedy. We will be visiting ancient Corinth, opulent city of merchants; Mycenae and the tomb of Agamemnon, the ill-fated king immortalized in Euripedes's tragedy; Epidaurus, the great amphitheatre where the plays of Euripedes and Aeschylus were performed; Olympia, the site of the original Olympic Games in 776 BC; Delphi, abode of the sacred Oracle on Mount Parnassus which is also the home of the legendary Muses; on to Kalambaka, famous for its olives, Greece's national tree; past the site of the famous battle of Thermopylae where 300 Spartans stood against an invading Persian horde in 480 BC; and back to Athens where some of you will embark on your three-day cruise of the Greek islands. Yes, gentleman with big nose? You are already exhausted keeping up with all this Historic culture even before trip has started? Sorry to say, but exhaustion is not on itinerary.

Today we start here with Athens, birthplace of democracy, in centre of which is hill of the Acropolis on top of which is famous Parthenon, temple of Athena, goddess of wisdom and learning, after which Athens is also named, which we visit tomorrow morning, eight a.m. sharp. In Historic Greece, culture begins early. However, this evening you may relax in Plaka, tourist area at foot of Acropolis—full of curio shops, cafes, restaurants etc. Are there also bars in Plaka? In Historic Greece foreigners were called barbarians because the sounds they made sounded like bar-bar. Gentleman with big nose is also going bar-bar. Is he barbarian? Ha ha. That is joke. On Historic tour, even our jokes are Historic.

Kali mera. Today we visit Acropolis and Parthenon, most famous historic monument in the world, built in the Golden Age of Pericles and standing now like the bleached ribcage of a vanished civilization against the azure sky. That is Historic poetic touch. Gentleman with big nose has something to say about poetic touch? No, he has something to say about how last evening in Plaka the kalamari he ordered was overpriced and underdone, the waiter rude, and the certified Madonna and Child Byzantine icon he purchased of suspect provenance because it showed baby Jesus in Pampers? Gentleman with big nose should remember Historic saying: Always look a Greek gift in the mouth—otherwise known as caveat emptor.

Now please to observe special quality of sunlight as it falls on broken column. It is this unique quality of light which is said to have given Historic Greeks their lucid philosophical insight. Also please to observe with lucid insight the three different capitals of columns which typify Historic Greek architecture: the Doric, plain and square; the Ionic, curly like a scroll or a ram's horns; and the Corinthian, ornate and shaped like leaves of acanthus plant. How will gentleman with big nose observe with lucid insight if it is Doric, Ionic or Corinthian columns which typify the architecture of the nearest public toilet which he is desperate to use? Please to observe that in Historic Greece, toilets, like food, are also always later.

Passing through the ruins of Corinth, once the trading centre of the world, we come to the ruins of Mycenaé with the beehive-shaped tomb of Agamemnon, which may not be Agamemnon's tomb at all because Agamemnon wasn't a man but a myth, except that in Historic Greece even myths have tombs. We will visit the ruins of Olympia, with the stadium, the temples of Zeus and Hera and the famous statue of Hermes by Praxiteles, fourth-century BC. But right now we are in the well-preserved ruin of the great amphitheatre of Epidaurus, which had a seating capacity of 14,000 and till today has such wonderful acoustics provided by its shape and its orientation to the surrounding hills that even a whisper made centre-stage can be heard clearly by all. What is it that the gentleman with the big nose whispered? That he is sick and tired of looking at old ruins and will someone please show him a nice new ruin? And his wife who whispered that all he had to do was go look in the mirror? On Historic Greece tour even domestic spats are Historic. Especially in Epidaurus, where they come in stereo.

Now we are in the rugged, haunted environs of Delphi, where lived the famed Oracle, the priestess to whom mighty kings and humble pilgrims came to discover the answers to the agonizing questions that beset them. The gentleman with the big nose would like to have discovered from the Oracle the answer to the agonizing question besetting him, namely as to why if in nearby Kalambaka there are three million olive trees there were only two olives in the Greek salad he ate for dinner last night? Some agonizing questions are best left Historically unanswered.

Passing through the battlefield of Thermopylae, and Thebes, the home of tragic Oedipus (Did the gentleman with the big nose mutter something about the original mama's boy?), we come back to Athens and the end of the Historic Greece tour. Any comments? The nice lady says that after the tour she can sit for an MA exam in Historic Greece? Thank you, madam. And her husband with the big nose? That Historic Greece is still all Greek to him? I'm afraid that as a humorist the gentleman with the big nose is not Historic; he is merely history.

* * *

A giant jelly made of Quink? I suggested. Bunny shook her head. A sorbet made of crushed sapphires, she said. She was right, as usual. I've never seen a sorbet of crushed sapphires. But if I had, I know it would look exactly like the Aegean Sea on which we were embarked on a three-day cruise, aboard the good ship *MTS Odysseus*.

We had thought that a cruise which took us to a scattering of the Greek islands would be the perfect way to unwind after the fascinating but hectic tour of Classical Greece we had undertaken. We were proved both right and wrong. The cruise was perfect. But in its own way equally as hectic as gadding about the mainland, getting a crash course in Hellenic antiquity. The *Odysseus*, a 12,000-ton vessel, offered a smorgasbord of entertainments—disco, swimming pool, casino, nightclub, cabaret acts, movies, conjuring shows, bingo sessions—which passengers were urged to sample.

But the main attraction on board was food. The *Odysseus*'s 12,000 tons patently referred not to the volume of water it displaced but to the mass of food ostensibly sought to be crammed down the collective maw of its passengers. Meals were included in the fare and there were four of them a day, with snacks sandwiched in between. No sooner had breakfast—thick Greek yoghurt, cereals, cold cuts, eggs, cheese, fruit etc—been burped than it was time for elevenses. And before you could say twelveses, buffet lunch was on—dolmades, vine leaves stuffed with rice; mousaka, an eggplant and cheese bake; kababs; salads; desserts. At 4.30 p.m. sharp came tea—sandwiches, cookies, cakes. Nine o'clock was dinner—like lunch, only more so. And if, after all that, you still felt peckish there was twenty-four-hour room service to cater to your hunger pangs.

To make up for all the free food on offer, the *Odysseus* charged pernicious prices for the accompanying booze, with the cheapest local retsina at fourteen US dollars a bottle. The tart white resin-flavoured wine was to be had for three dollars a litre on shore, and I suggested that at our first port of call we smuggle a couple of bottles on board and drink them in the privacy of our cabin.

This was overruled by executive fiat. What's the point of being on a cruise if you're going to skulk in your cabin like a mole, toping; we have to be on deck, sitting under the stars and looking at the sea, said Bunny. I didn't know moles toped; besides, there's a porthole in the cabin through which we can look at the sea, I pointed out helpfully. Yes, and the porthole's set so high you'd have to stand on the table to look out of it; come on Onassis, deck chalo and stop grumbling, said Bunny, leading the way.

So we sat on the deck and looked at blind Homer's 'wine-dark sea', and I figured the reason he had called it that: he too had to shell out fourteen bucks a pop for his plonk, poor bugger. The subconscious compulsions of gratis grub and overpriced drink haunted our vision and gave our metaphors a gastronomic tinge. The Aegean became an enormous jelly, or a vast sorbet. The island of Mykonos hove into view, a sun-dazzled outcrop of rock dotted with small square whitewashed houses like a carelessly strewn handful of sugar cubes. Please, no more edible descriptions, pleaded Bunny.

So I shut up trying to describe Mykonos and we went ashore to explore the little town which looked too tourist-brochure typical to be true, with its open-air cafes and tiny, blue-domed churches and the slow shuffle of cobbled lanes mazing like the steps of *Zorba the Greek*, dancing to the music of an unseen bouzouki. We sat at a table in a tavern and looked at the old disused windmills along the waterfront, some converted into gentrified residences, which resembled a row of ... Salt-and-pepper dispensers? suggested Bunny. And we knew that back on the *Odysseus* the dinner gong must be sounding. We were becoming positively Pavlovian in our conditioned responses.

It was the same at historic Rhodes, where we stopped next. We watched the flags fluttering above the crenellated walls of the Knights of St. John, the last of the crusaders, who built the citadel on the island from which they were finally expelled by Sultan Suleiman the Magnificent. In the glow of ageless afternoon, time seemed to coagulate, the amber patina of centuries coating the walled city like ... honey spread on warm toast? And we knew it must be teatime on board ship.

We anchored at Kusadasi on the so-called Turkish Riviera and visited Ephesus, said to be the largest excavated city of the ancient world. The guide took us past the library and the public baths to a broad stone-paved thoroughfare in which was set what is billed to be the oldest advertisement in the world: a foot pointing to a heart-shaped strawberry. It was a sign for a brothel, said the guide. Bunny nodded. Strawberry tart, probably what we'll get for dinner tonight, she sighed.

Cruise over, we disembarked at Piraeus, Athens's harbour. Bunny was thoughtful. You know, for all that hype about the free food on board, we didn't actually get to eat very much of it—we were too busy thinking and psyching ourselves out about it. We looked at the *Odysseus* with its cargo of our uneaten free food. I'll say this for the Greeks—they're the best cruise operators in the world, said Bunny. We looked at the *Odysseus* with its cargo of our empty bottles, at fourteen dollars a throw. With the accent on operators, I agreed ruefully.

Madrid Montage

People often ask me: Of the countries you've been to, which would you most like to revisit? I find this an invidious and unfair question. Like asking a parent: Which is your favourite child?

For of course, deep down, we all have our favourites. And, perhaps, mine is Spain. I hope this piece tells you why.

A word of warning, though: Unless you have nerves of steel, and a stomach to match, skip the bullfight. That's one Spanish experience I wouldn't like to experience again. And if you must go, pay the extra and sit on the shady side of the arena and not on the sunny side. A Spanish bullfight is traumatic enough without you collapsing from heatstroke.

Watching the rush-hour traffic thunder past the Plaza Mayor in Madrid, the larger-than-life statue of Don Quixote might well be moved to get off Rosinante and, like a lost tourist, approach an immaculately uniformed policeman to enquire as to where exactly he was. The response would reassure immediately. For, with a sombre ceremony evocative of the matador's arena or the flamenco floor, the official would turn, touch his cap and point out the way. This stylized ritual, so typically Spanish, fascinated us and sometimes even when we knew where we were, we would ask a policeman Por favore, Senhor. Donde este ... —just to see him do his bit as gravely as though it was something out of the last act of Carmen.

Smack in the centre of the Iberian peninsula, Madrid can be said to represent all of Spain—or none of it. According to Hemingway, it was the most Spanish of cities, precisely because it was such a hotchpotch, like a steaming platter of paella, rich with a random harvest of seafood, or the tempting displays of bite-size tapas in the glass cases of the tascas, the cafe-cum-bars, for which the city is justly famed.

Though that was a tale of another city, Hemingway's *A Moveable Feast* could as easily have been a title for Madrid. Perhaps the best aperitif to the city is a morning stroll through the Plaza Mayor, the vast, cobble-stoned square designed by Philip III in the seventeenth century. Framed by the classical symmetry of old grey stone buildings housing offices, shops and cafes, Plaza Mayor is like a painting slowly coming to life: cafe waiters setting out the round tables, fringing the square; ancient duennas in black, circled by the starling chatter of grandchildren; a wandering minstrel scattering casual notes from a guitar; office girls with the faces of Castilian Madonnas and staccato heels clacking counterpoint to a silent Bolero.

The crash of bombs, the screams of the mortally wounded, the roar of flames erupt in silence, off the painted surface of *Guernica*, arguably Picasso's greatest painting. The huge picture, with its agonized forms, takes up an entire wall in the special annexe to the Prado devoted to it. Though depicting the bombing of the village of Guernica during the Spanish Civil War, Guernica is more than a particular battleground; searing as napalm, its assault is that of apocalypse now.

After Guernica, the main building of the Prado, considered to be one of the finest art galleries in the world, is almost an anticlimax—for a moment. It takes a little while for perspectives to readjust, bruised senses to respond to other scenes, other faces of pain or joy. El Greco, Velasquez, Murillo, Tintoretto, Rubens, Breughel, and Ribera glow in the labyrinth of time. The Goya collection, beginning with cheerful pastoral scenes and becoming increasingly macabre, is like a fugue into madness, the final paintings as horrifying as *Guernica*. Born centuries apart, the two artists seem to reflect each other, with Spain bridging the chasm of years.

The early Goya is reflected in the great tapestries that drape the cold granite halls of the Escorial, the vast monastery-cum-palace built by Philip II to commemorate the Spanish victory over the French at Saint-Quentin in 1557. An hour's ride by train from Madrid, the looming grey pile is often described as 'the penal institution', and imprisons the visitor with an almost claustrophobic sense of history.

Though the guided tour is in Spanish, which we don't understand, the imagination weaves images as vivid as the famed tapestries that cloak the walls. Was it from this private chamber, as austere as its royal occupant, that Philip pursued his strict Roman Catholic policies which were to lead to a revolt in his Dutch domain? And was it in this chapel that he knelt in prayer, when, in 1588, he launched his great Armada against England with disastrous results?

If the Escorial is history petrified, the walled city of Toledo is a living museum-cum-souvenir mart for tourists. Some ninety kilometres from Madrid, the rocky, bush-covered landscape heaves up into a hill, on the crest of which soar battlements and towers, improbable as a Hollywood backdrop against which you expect, any moment, to see Charlton Heston materialize on horseback, in the avatar of El Cid.

Toledo, famed for its steel, has been forged in the crucible of conflict as Moor and Castilian strove for its possession. Once a citadel of Judaism and described as the 'European Jerusalem', Toledo lost its Jewish heritage to the flames of fanaticism lit by the Inquisition.

Today, the narrow, cobbled streets of Toledo are like a winding conveyor belt, carrying sightseers past the Gothic cavern of the Cathedral, the Alcazar citadel, the house of El Greco, and emporia crammed with mementos ranging from penknives to full suits of genuine imitations of medieval armour.

One candid camera snapshot of Toledo lingers long in the album of the mind: a middle-aged Japanese couple trudging uphill in the white heat of afternoon, under the curious gaze of locals lounging in the shade in somnolent siesta; the woman expostulating 'El Glecko, El Glecko!' to urge on her drooping companion, bowed under a burden of cameras and the tourist's do-or-die obligation to take in everything, no matter that one doesn't know what on earth one is looking at, or why.

Despite Hemingway's descriptions of bullfighting in *Death in the Afternoon* and *Fiesta*, we hadn't really known what we'd be looking at until the picador's lance thrust in through the muscle and bone of the bull. Till then, the whole thing had been a bit of a carnival; tawdry, but cheerful enough. Gaudy posters of cape-swirling matadors; families sharing bags of popcorn; the oom-pah-pah parade of the flamboyantly costumed toreros; the bull exploding into the ring like a black thunderbolt with horns; the banderilleros, graceful as ballet dancers, jabbing their long slender darts into the beast's back like festive streamers. At the centre of the danse macabre was the matador with his swirling cape, a swaying, spinning will-o'-the-wisp luring the stricken animal, taking ever greater risks to win the crowd's acclaim.

A hush fell at 'the moment of truth'. The slender sword a blazing sliver of sun in his hand, the matador provoked the charge, thrusting the blade in to the hilt as the bull blundered by, collapsed, unbelievably rose again to the tumult of the crowd, lurched forward to meet a second sword stroke, and a third, refusing to die as the stands went berserk, till its fighting heart finally gave out in a last spasm of fierceness, as the matador strutted around the arena, a macho marionette jerked by the applause of the spectators. What redeems bullfighting from being an act of senseless cruelty is the courage of the matador who, while dealing death, coolly faces it himself.

If bull, matador, and sand evoke the steel of Spain, the flamenco is its fire. We chose a nightclub in a narrow street off the Plaza Mayor and were shown to a table close to the small, low dais. The ripple of a guitar draws open an invisible curtain and the dancer steps on to the stage, high-held castanets clacking, feet tapping in arabesques of rhythm, that quicken to a catechism between dancer and musician, tempestuous and icy, seduction and challenge.

'And the clap of the hands
To the twirl and the swirl
Of the girl gone chancing,
Glancing, dancing,
Backing and advancing,
Snapping of the clapper to
the spin.
Out and in.'

In the flare of the spotlights, the movements become a shadow play, a dance to the music of time, beating faster and faster, till stage and room are spinning, racing to reach a crescendo that crashes down in stunning silence, a lull before the storm of applause.

On the flag-stoned plaza, we walked towards the distant lights of a late-night tasca, footsteps echoing the insistent pulse of the dance. We passed a policeman, but for once felt no need to seek directions. We knew exactly where we were: in the heart of Spain, in Madrid.

Scotch-taped

Years ago, in what was then called Calcutta, I knew a man with a secret sorrow: someone had presented him with a bottle of Royal Salute twenty-five-year-old Scotch whisky. The man kept the prized bottle locked up in a Godrej steel almirah.

Every now and then, on special occasions—a birthday, wedding anniversary, whatever—he would think of opening the bottle. But no event or celebration seemed special enough to merit such extravagance. The mystique of Scotch had subordinated his life.

I don't know what he finally did with the spirituous albatross around his neck. Leave it in his will for his children to deal with? Give it to a museum to put on display?

What he should have done of course was to go on the much travelled, and much touted Scotland 'whisky trail'. As Bunny and I did in 2001.

Lamont, our cab driver on Islay, told us about the man from San Francisco. Who flew all the way from there to London, from London to Glasgow, from Glasgow to the tiny landing strip on Islay, from where Lamont picked him up and drove him to the place which was the reason for his visit. He stayed there for six straight hours, and then drove back to the airstrip. He went back to San Francisco without even looking at the scenery; he had seen whatever he had wanted to see, said Lamont. Which was? Why, what else but the distillery where they make Laphroaig, arguably one of Scotland's most celebrated single malt whiskies. For the 'Friscan was one of the many millions the world over for whom Scotch—

particularly single malt Scotch—is not just a mere tipple but a holy grail, a consummation to be blessed.

Britain has two international marketing coups to its credit: the Royal family and Scotch whisky. Both are textbook examples of brand building. In the first case, an inbred bunch of chinless wonders were invested with the mystique of monarchy—in the face of the rising global tide of republicanism. And in the second case, a country-made hooch drunk by peasants who lived in a wet and boggy wilderness of hills and heather was turned into a liquid legend. Post-Diana, the royals look increasingly tacky. But Scotch—like the 'striding man' symbol on the Johnnie Walker bottle—goes marching on, despite a growing health consciousness which disapprovingly turns down an empty glass to most strong spirits.

What is the secret of the success of Scotch, the Gaelic 'usquebaugh' or 'water of life' from which the word whisky is derived? To find the answer, Bunny and I took up the much travelled 'whisky trail' at Inverness, gateway to the Scottish Highlands and to the Speyside region in which more than half of Scotland's seventy-odd distilleries cluster, thick as grains in an ear of barley.

The secret of Scotch? Ian Williams, manager of the Cardhu distillery—which apart from single malt Cardhu also makes the Johnnie Walker range, probably the best-known blended whiskies in the world—answered the question with a single word: fun. Forget the snobbery and the ritual associated with it, he said. Drink it anyway you like. So, is it okay then to have the stuff as a lot of people do in India—where, it is said, more Scotch is consumed every year than is made in Scotland—drowned in water, soda or even Coke? Why not? said the Cardhu man. And added poker-faced: I often have Johnnie Walker Red with Coke myself. He agreed, however, that a single malt should, ideally, be savoured neat or with, at most, a few drops of water to break the surface tension of the liquor and release its bouquet. A good Scotch must first be 'nosed' as a preliminary to actual tasting. Scotch might be 'fun', but apparently it is serious fun. Like listening to Jessie

Norman, or Nusrat Fateh Ali, sound made taste, and taste made sound, golden mellifluence undercut with a husky smokiness.

The manager explained the difference between grain whisky, generally made from corn, and single malts, made from barley. Grains, used in blended whisky, are distilled in a continuous, mass production process. Malts are made by first allowing the barley to germinate, or 'malt', then dry over burning peat, compacted turf, which imparts a smoky taste before the process of fermentation, brewing, and distillation begins. But grain whiskies ought not to be dismissed as assembly-line products as compared to the designer malts. For, in conjunction with malts, they can and do produce superlative blends which play like silent symphonies on the discerning palate.

Whisky, we were beginning to learn, is an education. And at Bruichladdich (pronounced Brook-lad-ick) distillery on Islay (pronounced Eye-la) they actually provide a live-in six-week diploma course in what might be called 'whiskyology'. Two hundred Japanese are said to have already signed on as the first batch. We flew to Islay, a 600-square-km speck of grit off the west coast of Scotland. Lamont picked us up at the landing strip and filled us in on the vital statistics of Islay: a population of little over 3000; one hospital; one high school; two policemen; and six distilleries, together employing some 119 people, the rest making a livelihood from sheep farming and catering to the 'bed and breakfast' needs of 'whisky tourists' like us. Lamont didn't 'inventorize' the spectacular landscape; he didn't need to. Stone-walled green fields ringed by the 360-degree arc of ocean; hills and valleys undulant as the surge of the sea, drifting with the white cumulus of sheep and splashed with the yellow sunshine of gorse and the exuberance of purple heather; an immensity of light and sky filled with a silence as eloquent as the space between two heartbeats.

We stopped at the Laphroaig (pronounced La-froig) distillery, by the rock-ribbed shoreline. Laphroaig is billed as being Prince Charles's favourite whisky, but Bunny and I were prepared to forgive it that. The name, as Ian Henderson, the manager, told us, means 'The beautiful hollow by the broad bay'. He took us through the by now familiar litany of whisky making: the malting of the barley, the peat smoking, the mashing, the distillation, and, of course, the addition of the all-important, crystal clear natural spring water that is the unique ingredient of all Scotch.

But I was no longer really listening. Not out of boredom, far from it, but because I had finally intuited the real secret of Scotch. It's a conspiracy. The makers will tell you about the barley, or corn as the case may be, about the copper stills and the oaken ageing casks. But those mundane, mechanical details are just a cover-up. For the canny Scots have somehow managed to ensnare the remoteness of sea and sky, scudding cloud and misty rain, the flame of gorse and the livid bruise of heather, and, in some untold alembic, distilled it into the essence of their bleak and beautiful land.

Laphroaig gives you a clue to this. When you buy a bottle, you get a card on which you put your name and send to the distillery which then leases you in perpetuity a square foot of Islay turf. The 'rent' you receive is in the form of a free dram of Laphroaig whenever you visit Islay.

As Lamont dropped us off at the airstrip, I knew why his earlier passenger, the San Franciscan, hadn't bothered to look at the view. He knew he was taking it all back with him in his luggage.

Back home in Gurgaon, I crack open the bottle of special fifteen-year-old Laphroaig that Ian Henderson very generously presented us. I take a sip. And from my Jaipuri carpet blooms irrepressibly a sprig of purple heather. I drink not to Scotland; I drink Scotland itself (pronounced itself).

A Pint-sized Ulysses

We had long wanted to go to Ireland. We finally made it in 1991. As a bonus, the day we reached Dublin was Bloom Day, 16 June, which commemorates the twenty-four-hour odyssey of Leopold Bloom, the protagonist of James Joyce's epic, Ulysses, *through the city. Each year, Dublin celebrates Bloom Day with a bewildering host of events, both planned and extempore.*

How am I going to write about all this? I asked myself. And decided I'd try my hand at some Joycean stream-of-consciousness. Stream-of-unconsciousness, critics have pointed out. To which I reply: Don't blame me. Blame the Guinness. It's a wonder it isn't stream-of-comatose.

And yes I said yes I will yes, which of course are the last words, as well as the first, almost, of Molly Bloom's sixty-two-page, single-sentence, punctuation-less, orgasmic, life-affirming monologue which concludes James Joyce's mock heroic masterpiece, *Ulysses*, which details the one-day odyssey of Leopold Bloom, a Dublin-based advertising-space salesman, as on 16 June 1904, he traverses the city and, like Homer's hero, encounters ogres and sirens, friends and betrayers, except in their latter-day, mundane avatars, on a mythic journey re-enacted each year on Bloom Day, 16 June, in Dublin where Bunny and I were this year, retracing the meandering footsteps of Leopold, Joyce's Everyman, who, as the writer tells us, ate with relish the inner organs of beasts and fowls, though Philip McDonagh, the current Irish ambassador to India, corrected me that it was another Joyce character, Buck Mulligan, who enjoyed these delicacies, but now I must make a re-correction, having revisited Joyce in situ, so to speak, that in fact it was Bloom who favoured such fare, but knowledgeable and helpful chap that he is, Philip did recommend his favourite Dublin pub, Doheny and Nesbitt, an incomparable watering-hole in a city famed for pubs, where Bunny and I stopped to have a drink and where I felt it apt to echo Molly Bloom's words, And yes I said yes I will yes, to the barman's offer of another pint of Guinness, the black, velvet smooth 'foaming ebon ale', the Irish national drink, which, along with Joyce, is one of Ireland's highest profile exports, 10,000,000 glasses of the stuff being downed daily in 151 countries round the world, for the goodness that's in it, to be sure, and as I sipped my pint I could taste on my tongue the irreverent, yeasty music of Joyce's prose which with bitter-sweet irony took over and transfigured the English language, much like our own Rushdie was to do some eighty-odd years later, one of the many sub-textual comparisons, social, political, and cultural, that the Indian visitor to Ireland is tempted to make, at the risk of specious metaphor, between the two countries both of which won freedom from the same colonial power after much bloodshed and bitter internecine strife whose final course is still to run in both our cases, Ulster in theirs, partition and its repercussions, including Kashmir, in ours, though rightly finical commentators would point out many fallacies in such facile comparisons, but that being said and done there's no denying that the Irish are probably the friendliest folk on earth, particularly towards Indians, and especially in pubs, which are places to drink in, so they are, but much more than that are still centres of the turning world, quotidian repositories of a resonant oral tradition of ballad and song and legend and story, topped with a frothy head of Irish blarney, which turns the madness of history into a narrative as fluent as the river Liffey which, many-bridged stream of consciousness, runs through Dublin and murmurs to those who stop to hear of the pain and passion of Ireland, of Brian Baru, the last of the great Irish kings in

the eleventh century; of the coming of the Vikings; of the
colonization by the English; of the disastrous Battle of the
Boyne in 1690; of Cromwell's massacres which make
Jalianwala Bagh pale in comparison; of the great potato
famine of the 1840s, which decimated the population; of the
infamous 'coffin ships' that sailed from Galway to America
freighted with passengers who died of starvation and whose
corpses were flung overboard mid-voyage; of the great Irish
diaspora which today accounts for the fact that there are
some five million Irish in Ireland and over twelve times that
number abroad, from America to Australia and points in
between; of the Easter Rising of 1916 when Yeats's 'terrible
beauty' of rebel martyrdom was born; of the fratricidal civil
war which led to an amputated liberty; of Ireland's no less
than four literary Nobel laureates, its claim to being western
Europe's biggest per capita buyer and reader of books, and
its pre-eminence in the IT software industry, all of which
eloquently rebut the English caricature of the 'thick Mick'
and the good-for-nothing Paddy layabout, a canard
handsomely refuted by Dublin itself, fair city of sweet Molly
Malone, elegant Georgian architecture, cobble-stoned Temple
Bar, the verdant hush of St Stephens Green, the fashionable
shops and tea rooms of pedestrian-only Grafton Street, the
ancient stone tranquillity of Trinity College, home to the
illuminated 1000-year-old *Book of Kells*, one of the oldest
books in the world, our guidebook tells us, as Bloom-like
Bunny and I criss-cross the eminently walkable city, pausing
every now and again for a fortifying pint, or perhaps two, in
one of the numberless pubs, each of which extends the
traditional Gaelic invitation, Cead mile failte, a hundred
thousand welcomes, not the least of them being the Dawson
Lounge on Dawson Street, billed as Dublin's smallest pub,
but perhaps with the largest heart, the evening Bunny and I
are there when Martin, a prodigal son briefly returned from
Nova Scotia, buys drinks for the house, all eight of us, Bunny
and me specially included, for no reason other than 'it's a
right grand thing to do, so it is, I saw it once in a movie', and

then comes over and kisses Bunny three times and shakes my hand, also three times on the principle of equal opportunity, that it seems impossibly churlish to leave, not just the pub, but Dublin itself, but leave we do to take a coach right across the island from east to west, to seaside Galway, where we base ourselves to explore first the granite remoteness of Connemara, where valleys between windswept hills shelter lakes as silver and sudden as shards of a shattered mirror, and then we wheel south to County Clare, green and suppliant under the ceaseless caress of her lover, the rain, which follows us back to Dublin, insistent as the haunting refrain of Patrick Kavanagh's poem, 'If ever you go Dublin Town/ On Pembroke Road look out for my ghost/ Dishevelled, with shoes untied,/ Playing through the railings with little children/ Whose children have long since died', which is as good a toast as any to end a mini-odyssey of discovery, a pint-sized one, if you prefer, which knows that for all the pangs of leave-taking, if in its beginning is its end, in its end is also a beginning, a Joycean affirmation, a yes I said yes I will yes

Rocky Mountain Low

We first visited America during its bicentennial celebrations in 1976. We've been back several times since then. The trip to Denver described in the following piece was in 1994.

We haven't been to the US after 9/11 and the emergence of George 'Dubya' Bush as the self-appointed custodian of global peace and democracy. As 'Rocky Mountain Low' suggests, the US of A is 'aah-some' enough without Bushbaby making it even more so.

When Bunny and I visited the US, Omarr, Bunny's college-going Yankee cousin, gave me a crash course in idiomatic American. 'Lesson number one: Say aah-some,' said Omarr.

'Aah-some,' I duly repeated.

'Congratulations, you've just learnt to speak American,' said Omarr.

'You mean that's all there is to American?' I persisted.

'Yup, that's about it,' said Omarr. 'Sure, you got guys who also say "Hi", and "How're you doin?", and "Have a nice day", but that's like dialects, you know? You just stick to aah-some, you'll get along fine.'

'But what does aah-some mean?' I asked.

'It means anything you want it to: Big, huge, great, fantastic, fabulous, terrific, wonderful, real cool, groovy, humongous, super excellent like in really bad, you know?' explained Omarr.

'Aah-some,' I muttered the magical mantra in wonderment.

'Now you're rapping, man,' said Omarr. 'Go get 'em, Tiger.'

As I went to go get 'em, I reflected that America was indeed an aah-some place. Other nations strive to be regional powers;

the US is Globo-cop. Other countries flex their nuclear arsenals; America flexes Arnold Schwarzenegger. Other economies owe money to the World Bank; America is the World Bank and the money it owes to itself has created a fiscal chasm after which the Grand Canyon is modelled. Aah-some.

Everything about America is aah-some. We went to a sandwich bar in Stamford, Connecticut. The girl behind the counter placed in front of me something that looked like the entire contents of the larder of the *Titanic* which had made it the *Titanic*, with dill pickle on the side. 'I asked for a sandwich, not a year's food supply to Rwanda,' I said. 'It *is* a sandwich,' said the girl. 'It's our regular twelve-inch Hero Subway.'

'Aah-some,' I said by way of grace.

As I ingested my regular twelve-inch Hero Subway I pondered on the truly aah-some part of America. America is a big country—three times the size of India—yet wherever you go in this huge great land, from sea to shining sea, everything seems aah-somely the same. McDonald's seems the same as Subway which seems the same as Pizza Hut which seems the same as Kentucky Fried Chicken which seems the same as Taco Bell which seems the same as 32 Flavours of Baskin Robbins ice-cream, all mass-produced in the same eternal shopping mall, forever and ever, aah-men.

'Can't we go someplace in America which is different from America?' I asked.

'Try the Rockies,' suggested Juju, Omarr's mom.

The Rocky Mountains. Of course, that was it. If American sandwiches looked like mountains, what would American mountains look like? Imagination boggled. So, packing bag, baggage, and boggled imaginations, Bunny and I caught a plane to Denver, Colorado, the famous Mile High city, so called because it stands exactly 5280 feet above sea level.

From the seventeenth floor of the Comfort Inn in downtown Denver we looked at the towering stone canyons of the Wall Street of the West, where the TV series *Dynasty* is said to have been shot. There was something odd about Denver, and it took me a moment to place it. The city had hotels, offices, mansions, parks, museums, and historic sites, but seemingly no people. Maybe they were all playing golf at Denver's thirty-eight golf courses.

'It's Sunday,' said Bunny. 'Wait till Monday morning rush hour.'

The next morning we went down to look at Denver's rush hour. Three cars stopped on our left at a red light; three cars passed on our right at a green light. Then the lights changed and Denver's rush hour was over. 'Aah-some,' said Bunny. It was catching.

We took a coach tour of the Rocky Mountains. We drove through Cripple Creek, which started the Colorado gold rush in 1890, and passed Golden where liquid gold is produced by Coors who, in the world's biggest brewing plant, make two million gallons of beer a month.

The road wound upward through woods of aspen and pine, high above the dusty plains which Bob, our driver, told us were once covered by a seething, hairy sea of buffaloes. Pioneer wagon trains coming west had to halt for eight to ten days to let a single herd pass, all 200 miles of it. We didn't see any buffalo. 'What happened to them?' asked a passenger. 'They got killed,' said Bob, and told us how Buffalo Bill Cody once shot 4400 of the animals in a single month, supplying meat to the railroad being built.

The legend of buckskinned Buffalo Bill Cody—archetypal frontiersman and tamer of the wilderness—looms higher than the Rockies. Wells Fargo rider, buffalo hunter, Native Indian fighter, and cavalry scout, William F. Cody, who toured Europe and England with his Wild West show and who was presented to Queen Victoria, died in penury. In exchange for his debts being discharged by a Denver businessman, he agreed on his deathbed to be buried on nearby Lookout Mountain. The good citizens of the town of Cody, Wyoming, however, took exception to this expropriation of the mortal remains of their favourite son and one night a band of them raided the grave and took Buffalo Bill to bury him in their town. The Denverites went and fetched him right back, posting the National Guard over the grave. But the enterprising Codyans zicked Buffalo Bill again, and the Denverites had to get him back once more, this time pouring sixteen tons of concrete on the grave to ensure that the itinerant incumbent stayed in place.

We stopped to take pictures of Bill's grave. At the souvenir shop I bought a stick of ersatz buffalo meat and raised a silent salute to the man who almost single-handedly turned a species into salami sausage.

We reached Berthoud Pass, two miles high in the Rockies. We were smack in the heart of America, on the top of the Continental Divide where, theoretically, if you peed on one side of a pine tree, part of you would end up in the Atlantic, and if on the other side of the tree, in the Pacific. I was about to try this out when Bob asked me if I was feeling the altitude, and I said no, I was used to it, and soon we got talking about the Himalayas. It turned out that Bob in his younger days had been to Tibet. He told me about one time in Lhasa when it was so cold you could drink boiling tea and not feel it. And I told him about a blizzard at Fotu La, on the Srinagar-Leh highway, where the snow fell upward, so high were we above the storm clouds. Pretty soon the other passengers stopped looking at the Rockies to listen to us, as our tales got taller and taller.

Back in Stamford, people asked me about the Rockies. 'Must have been aah-some,' they suggested. 'They were indeed,' I replied. 'More some than aah.'

Acapulco Dreaming

Did Bunny and I really get there? In 1983? After some thirty-six hours of travel time from Calcutta and five aircraft changes? Or did I just dream it all up?

Quite possible. But for one thing. Somewhere deep in Bunny's wardrobe lies buried a T-shirt bearing the legend: I sunned my buns in Acapulco.

On the sun-drenched beach at Acapulco a man walks by me wearing a T-shirt that says 'Alaska '82'. I blink and wonder if I'm suffering from jet lag induced by the thirty-six-hour hopping flight from Calcutta, via London, New York, and Mexico City, to this millionaire's playground on the Pacific coast of Mexico.

A lissom girl with the merest hint of a bikini sways past. All around me is picture-postcard land. A golden horseshoe beach fringed by palm trees and a panorama of luxury hotels and apartment blocks backing on to rolling hills; a blue-green sea with a foaming surf and a festive assortment of pleasure boats, waterskiers, parasailers, and bathers. It doesn't take much to imagine Elvis Presley singing *Fun in Acapulco* as background music for the scene.

Fun, of all sorts, both innocent and otherwise, is now the sole reason for Acapulco's existence. It wasn't always so. In the language of the Nahuatal Indians who were the original inhabitants, Acapulco means 'the place of the cane in the water'. The Spanish colonizers, taking advantage of its excellent natural harbour, made it an important seaport and shipbuilding centre. Fragrant spices and gossamer fabrics were imported from Asia in exchange for Mexican silver. The prosperous trade attracted both wealthy financiers and pirates, giving Acapulco a colourfully chequered history.

After the Mexican War of Independence (1810–1821), the Spanish connection was severed and Acapulco became a sleepy, obscure little fishing village. Then it was 'discovered' as an ideal get-away-from-it-all by Hollywood stars like Errol Flynn, John Wayne, and Frank Sinatra, and Acapulco's tide turned once again. It became the place for the international jet set— a tropical paradise with a mean annual temperature of 80 degrees F, an idyllic bay, Marguerita cocktails on tap, and an accommodating Deity with whom the local authorities seemed to have struck a deal that it would rain—if it did at all—only at night, just to keep the grass nice and green for the golfers.

Today, with a resident population of 600,000, Acapulco gets on an average 25,000 visitors a month, has 500 hotels and, in the new part of the city at least, has about as much flavour of authentic Mexico as the steaks and martinis served in the American-style bars and restaurants that line the neon-lit Avenue Miguel Alimar, the 'main drag' of the town.

My first impression of Acapulco, like most subsequent ones, was of vague unreality. Light-headed with fatigue and jet lag, Bunny and I got to our hotel room at three o'clock in the morning, local time. A steady roar from outside drowned the gentle hiss of air-conditioning. 'Bloody hell! How do they expect us to sleep with those damn trucks thundering by?' I muttered.

I stepped onto the balcony and froze at one of the most stunning sights I have seen. Instead of a highway heavy with traffic that I'd expected, what greeted me in the late moonlight was a sweeping curve of phosphorescent surf pounding in on a ghostly crescent of beach nine floors below me. From the dark horizon, the lights of an anchored ship seemed like signals from a distant planet which were reflected and answered a thousand-fold in the twinkling cobweb of luminosity that veiled the encircling skyscrapers in the glowing mist.

'I don't believe this,' I said, 'I just don't believe it,' and we poured drinks, sat in the balmy breeze of the balcony, and watched the moon fade and the darkness drain into the mauve sea. As the horizon lightened, a boat cut across the bay wheeled over by gulls and the first surf riders emerged like priests of some ancient rite to celebrate the genesis of a new day. I still couldn't believe it.

There is lot that is unbelievable about Acapulco as we find out on our first day. After driving through old Acapulco, past the Byzantine cathedral, the seventeenth-century San Diego Fort built to keep pirates at bay, Frank Sinatra's villa perched on a hill in picturesque and exclusive isolation, and the disused bullring deserted by the toreros who have all gone to play jai alai in America which is more paying and considerably less dangerous than fighting bulls, we come to the cliffs of Quebrada, home of the famous divers.

On the spectators' platform there is breathless silence as a lean, sun-bronzed young man poises at the edge of the 140-foot cliff. A dizzy plunge below, the sea surges in and out of a narrow, rock-choked inlet. The young man must time his dive to coincide with the crest of an incoming wave or he will smash himself on the rocks below. A wave rushes in and the diver swoops down in a graceful arc. For a timeless moment his body seems to hang in the air, an upside-down crucifix, before it knifes into the raging water. As the viewers crowd to the platform railing, the diver re-emerges to wave at them. Already, another diver, having prayed before a small statue of the Virgin, is taking his position on the cliff top.

The La Quebrada divers are said to be a unique Acapulco tourist attraction. There are just six of them, comprising a closely guarded guild. Each outgoing member nominates his successor, generally a relative. We are told that although there have been a few broken bones from time to time, there has never been a fatality. The divers are subsidized by the government and add to their earnings by the tips tourists give them.

The show over, we file past the grinning, dripping divers waiting for us on the steps. 'You like? You like, senor, senorina?' Guiltily, I thrust a 200-peso note into a wet hand. I feel shamefaced, a latter-day Roman paying for the thrill of seeing a gladiator gamble with death.

The bus takes us in a wide circle through the scrub-covered Sierra Madre hills to the super-luxury colony of Las Brisas, The Breezes—seventy-two villas each with its own private swimming pool, candy-striped jeep, and wall-to-wall millionaires. From up here, the old part of the city with its barrios, crowded alleys, and open-air markets is a remote blur. The cost of a two-week stay in Las Brisas, we are told, would keep a local family in moderate comfort for a year.

Invited to dinner at the penthouse restaurant on the twenty-third floor of the Hyatta Excelaris, we are so mesmerized by the view through the plate-glass wall—the curving bay embraced by the tall cliffs of the condominiums clouded in jewelled cobwebs of lights—that we hardly notice what we eat.

Mandy and Bob, two young Canadian journalists we have met, insist we go to a disco. Acapulco's discotheques are world famous and the current rage is a place called Baby O, which is where we end up. Mandy, who seems to know the scene, somehow gets us in despite the queues at the door. We walk into a solid wall of sound interspersed with thunderbolt flashes of strobe lighting. The under-lit dance floor is a single, seething organism twitching its myriad limbs to the galvanic beat.

We squeeze into the mass and I discover that you don't have to dance, in fact you can't. All you do is stand there and the press of bodies heaves and jerks you about in the appropriate motions. It's like being part of a giant blancmange or a cell in a great amoeba which existed at the dawn of evolution.

The next day, we flee the tourist beat and seek the folkways of the back alleys of Acapulco. We find a dhaba-style eatery and sit down at a wooden table. The proprietor greets us with a stream of the local Spanish which always sounds to me something like a cross between the Gettysburg address and the sales spiel of a Sindhi shopkeeper. Neither of us understands a word. Since Indians tend to look confusingly like Mexicans, or vice versa if you prefer, we are often mistaken for indigenes. 'No hablo Espanol,' we say, 'no speak Spanish, Indianos, from India.' We indicate great distances, faraway shores.

Our genial host beams in sudden comprehension. 'Ah, Indianos! India si, si. Gandhi, eh? Si, si!' With the Mahatma, as reincarnated on celluloid by Dickie Attenborough, as our referee, we get effusive service. Heaped platters of enchiladas, tortillas, frijoles, and chilli con carne arrive at the table. Mexican cuisine is very reminiscent of north-Indian food. The basic preparation, the tortilla, is like a cornflour chappati. Stuffed with meat and crisp fried it becomes a taco, filled with cheese and vegetables and lightly grilled it turns into an enchilada.

The chilli con carne could pass for a keema-rajma and no questions asked. We wash it down with chilled 'cerveza', or beer. I ask for a shot of tequila, the clear, cactus-based drink which is the true distillation of the Mexican ethos. It looks, smells, and tastes a little like Goan feni and is liquid dynamite.

Emboldened, I ask for mescal, made from the juice of the same plant from which the hallucinogenic drug mescaline is obtained. Mescal is to tequila what VSOP cognac is to granny's cherry brandy, and Bob and Mandy have told me that the makers of the best mescal put into the bottle a live worm whose death juices impart a subtle twist to the taste.

But the proprietor has no mescal to offer, with or without worms, so we pay the agreeably modest bill and stroll out onto the street full of urchins, beggars, stray dogs, old women carrying squawking chickens, and stalls selling everything from sombreros and ponchos to silverware and sticky sweets. A typical Indian bazaar scene.

Bunny stops at a vendor selling bright T-shirts bearing the legend 'I sunned my buns in Acapulco'. The accompanying design showing a curvaceous feminine posterior leaves no doubt what part of the anatomy is being referred to. The man asks for an outrageous price and Bunny begins to haggle with him in sign language. Fortunately, I happen to read the label 'Made in Pakistan' and we leave the salesman wondering what those two Mexican-looking foreigners suddenly found so hysterically funny.

We are back in the world of tourists. From Caleta Beach we take a glass-bottomed boat that passes over the underwater bronze shrine of the Virgin of Guadalope before reaching Roqueta Island on whose rocky soil bars and discos flourish like exotic blooms. Sitting at a table in an outdoor café, sipping 'cocolocos'—coconuts laced with tequila—we have a wrap-around view of Acapulco Bay.

The improbably blue sky, the hills sprinkled with cubist patterns of villas, the kaleidoscope of parasailers, waterskiers, and surf boarders, the glass and steel towers of the skyscrapers, flashing secret messages to the setting sun, make it look like an opening shot of a Hollywood film of high-living romance and intrigue. We wonder what it must feel like to be an Acapulcan, to actually live in and not just visit a place that looks and acts like a movie set all the time.

We'll never know the answer to that one. The next day we are at the airport, waiting for our flight out. But Acapulco has a last surprise for us. Mandy and Bob are there with a farewell present: a bottle of mescal, complete with a fat worm curled up inside and slowly spinning as we hold the bottle up against the sun and turn it in disbelief.

'Take a sip, and wherever you are you'll be back in Acapulco again,' they say, wishing us goodbye as we board the plane taking us back from never-never land to the real world.

A postscript from London: We open the bottle of mescal in the doll's-house parlour of a semi-detached in British suburbia. Outside, it's weepy, grey English weather. The friends we are staying with look on in fascinated horror as I pour four small measures.

'Are you sure it's safe to drink?' they ask apprehensively.

'I'll be the guinea pig,' I reply as I hold my breath and take a sip. It goes down smooth as silk, erupts in a fireball that makes me gasp. Suddenly, a great golden sun blazes over Norbury, SW 16.

'Here's to Acapulco,' I say and knock back the rest of the glass.

Cuba Libre

Hemingway? Graham Greene? Martin Cruz Smith's Havana Bay? The music of the Buena Vista Social Club?

Actually, it was Sachi, our friend who lives in Toronto, who got us to go to Cuba. Go there, you'll love it, said Sachi. So we went there, in 2002. And we did love it. Perhaps too much. For as we found out, Cuba can break your heart.

When Sachi read this piece, he said it made him want to go back to Cuba. One good turn ...

If cities were people, Havana would be Don Quixote. Ragged knight errant, driven by hopeless chivalry to tilt against the windmills of his madness, riding a broken-down nag, forever in love with the raddled seductress of revolution. If cities were music, Havana would be jazz played on a scratched record, the needle of time skittering across the grooves of past and present in random riffs.

The broad promenade of the Malecon skirts Havana bay, a panoramic sweep that visually echoes Bombay's Marine Drive of fifty years ago. Elegant Spanish colonial mansions and neo-modern tower blocks, windows heavy-lidded as a mafioso's eyes, moulder like decaying cheese under the rancid sun. American cars of 1950s vintage—Chevys, Cadillacs, Buicks—cruise like benign sharks along avenues of anachronism. There is an air of derelict grandeur, a tuxedo blotched with mildew. On the stroke of midnight, New Year's Eve, 1958, a young guerrilla called Fidel Castro overthrew the corrupt Batista regime and stopped time, which has yet to start again.

Cuba is the last, lost romance of the Left, and the iconography of the 'revolucion' is everywhere: on walls, posters, murals. A man with a beard, a beret, and a dream. Fidel the Father, and Che his Son. But there is another, equally abiding presence. Bunny and I feel it as we walk along the cobbled lanes of Havana Vieja, Old Havana, with its deeply colonnaded eighteenth-century buildings, its flagstoned squares and street-side cafes where gypsy women in colourful skirts wheedle coins from tourists.

I sense him following us through the drifting crowds of people, through the elliptical swing of salsa music. I turn to face him. He is big, bull shouldered, grizzle bearded. Why are you trailing us? I ask him. Trailing you? You're trailing *me*. Why don't you leave me alone, I've been dead forty-two years, says the ghost of Papa Hemingway and disappears to have a mojito cocktail in his favourite bar, the Bodeghita del Media, whose walls are spider-webbed with thousands of signatures of everyone from Marquez to Salvador Allende.

Papa's right, as always. Urged by guidebooks and the locals, tourists follow Hemingway's spoor with the tenacity of bloodhounds. Papa's love affair with the country is well known; it began with big-game marlin fishing and went on to embrace all things Cuban. There are pictures of him with an incredibly young Castro, the two of them grinning together as if at some secret joke.

Papa seemed to have gone everywhere in Cuba, and wherever he went has been turned into a shrine. Room 511 in the Ambos Mundos hotel where he began writing *The Sun Also Rises* has been preserved the way it was when he lived in it, his typewriter on the table. Tourists peer in reverence, at two dollars a look. At the Floridita bar you can have a daiquiri—or better still, a Hemingway Special (rum, grapefruit juice, soda) specially invented in his honour—and watch the Papa clones standing at the bar and looking more real than the real thing.

We take a coco taxi (like an Indian auto-rickshaw but far more comfortable) to the nearby fishing village of Cojimar, the setting for *The Old Man and the Sea*, which won Hemingway the Nobel Prize. The old fisherman on whom the protagonist was based died in January this year, aged 104. We go to see his small, blue-painted house, No. 209.

Our driver is Daniel, young, blond, talkative in broken English. Daniel's coco taxi, like everything else in Cuba, is owned by the state. Daniel has to earn and give the government fifty-two US dollars every day for the privilege of driving it. In return, the government gives him a salary of 150 pesos (less than six dollars) a month. Of course, almost everything is free, or virtually so—schools, housing, medicare—but even then it's tough going. Daniel, divorced, has a two-year-old daughter. She always wanting candy, ice-cream, very expensive, says Daniel with an indulgent smile.

To meet his daily fifty-two-dollar quota, Daniel has to work very long hours. His unemployed younger brother babysits Daniel's daughter. Daniel is a Catholic. Is he also a communist? He seems astonished by the question. Of course he is a communist. What else would anyone, could anyone, be?

In La Terraza bar in Cojimar, Daniel takes a snapshot of Bunny and me sitting under a picture of Hemingway. He says tomorrow he can take us to Casa Hemingway, the house where Papa lived and which is now a museum. And then there's his yacht, *Pinar*, and the Marina Hemingway, named after him.

Unfortunately, the next day everything is closed, including the Hemingway Museum. Someone had the audacity to suggest that, perhaps, forty-odd years after the revolucion maybe the system needed a few reforms. So in response, Fidel gets together eight million of his followers and closes down the whole country.

Does this sort of thing happen often? Oh yes, all the time, a diplomat in Havana assures me. It's ruining the country, which is already bankrupt.

I don't know about the country, but I worry about Daniel. How will he meet his fifty-two-dollar target for the day, without which he can't keep his coco taxi? How will he buy his favourite two-year-old the ice-cream she demands? How will he remain both a good communist and a good father?

How can he remain a good Cuban? Only by fleeing to America, country of the beloved Papa, country of hated imperialism? And I think about those pictures of the two amigos together, Fidel and Papa. One of them killed himself forty years ago, and turned himself into an undying myth. The other has lived on, embalmed in his own legend so that it seems he can no longer die, even though his obsessive revolucion turns his country into a mausoleum for a lost cause.

And I wonder. If the two friends could meet again today, which one could tell the other that it was he who had the easier end.

The revolucion began with a bang, a New Year firework dazzling the sky with brilliance. In a single year, 1960, a special drive made Cuba 100 per cent literate. Even today, the country's health care is the envy of more developed societies, and its sporting achievements are impressive. But almost everything else seems to have come unstuck, particularly after the dissolution of the USSR, Cuba's chief financial sponsor.

When Bunny and I were there, the whole country—offices, schools, museums, everything—was suddenly shut down for three days. The reason? El Presidente was going to announce some 'important political reforms' on television and he wanted his people to stay at home and ponder over his message without extraneous distractions. That's how the revolucion works—by not working. Almost nothing works in Cuba. It is as if efficiency were a crime against the revolucion. In restaurants (like almost all other businesses, barring a few joint ventures, restaurants are state-run—except for a handful of privately owned 'paladares' which by law cannot seat more than twelve customers at a time) waiters don't wait. It's the customers who do—for food that never seems to come. Toilets don't flush. Taps don't run. Most Cubans earn no more than ten US dollars a month, less than a third of the cost of a single lobster dinner for a tourist.

Much of this is blamed on the throttling US economic embargo, condemned by most countries. The conflict between the US and Cuba is not between two countries but two faiths—individual liberty versus collective emancipation: together we are greater than the sum of our separate egos. Who's right? Since the revolucion, thousands of Cubans have voted with their rafts, risking the hazardous sea crossing to the US. Some, like four-year-old Elian, have hit international headlines. There has been no reverse mass migration.

But those who choose to stay—or have no choice—grin and bear it: proud to be Cubans, and to hell with anyone who says different. Yes, nothing works in Cuba, except for the indomitable gallantry of its people. Over the years, black ex-slaves and their former white masters have commingled to create a handsome, honey-coloured fraternity of races. There is an infectious camaraderie in the air: We may wear rags, but they are the glad rags of celebration. Barefoot kids play jubilant baseball, using castaway wooden staves for bats.

Every day, and through most of the night, the strains of samba and salsa pour out of private homes and cafes, like the rum with which Havana's bartenders claim to make as many as 100 different cocktails. Can't afford a drink? No problem. The music's everywhere and it's free. Everywhere else in the world the Party is over; here the party's just begun.

But though Cuba has banished biological racism, it has entrenched an economic apartheid. Cubans must earn and spend emaciated Third World pesos; visitors are obliged to buy, often the same goods and services, only in superfatted First World dollars. The pneumatic hiss of tourist coaches disgorging passengers immediately attracts a swarm of 'jineteros', hustlers trying to sell cheap cigars, cheap food, cheap sex, cheap anything.

At a street cafe, an old man tries to 'sell' us a plastic pen that won't write. Another, with nothing else to 'sell', pokes out his glass eyeball with a stick and holds it out to us on the palm of his hand. Uno dollar, si? Give me a dollar and I'll take my eye out again for you. Can he see the cruel irony of the 'eternal and glorious triumph of the revolucion'? Can you see anything except hope for a tip when your eye is lying on your out-thrust hand? Yet, in the midst of grotesque poverty, there is incredible generosity. On the ferry from Havana Vieja to Casablanca across the harbour, an anonymous young man, seeing us take out US cents for our tickets, holds a cautionary finger to his lips. Shh! Pretend you're Cuban; I'll pay for you in Cuban centavos.

We try to repay him, thank him, but with a smile and a shrug he's gone. Why did he do it? Bunny and I ask each other. Why? Because he's as much a product of Fidel's Cuba as the man with the glass eye. Because when you have nothing else, what can you give but the inexhaustible wealth of brotherhood? We're all comrades, all together. So what if the boat we're on is called the *Titanic*.

Perhaps this is what makes Fidel so dangerous to his opponents, who at the last count had made some 600 failed attempts on his life. For Fidel represents not reality, but an idea. A gesture, an attitude. And even if they had succeeded, on each one of those 600 occasions, they would have killed him but they still wouldn't have killed his idea, unworkable and unrealizable though it may be. In fact, its futility may be its greatest strength: If I can't make it happen, you can't say it failed—only that *I* did.

Stuck like a jaunty cigar in the mouth of the Caribbean, Cuba continues to confront the US Goliath. Come on, hombre. Make my day. Mano a mano. For sheer machismo, it's an unparalleled act. Forty-three years on, Fidel's revolucion is on its last legs. But like Hemingway's Old Man it remains a testament to an unyielding truth: I can be destroyed; but I can never be defeated.

In the amber afterglow of dusk, I take a last walk along the Malecon and raise a toast to Cuba libre: Salud to its pride, its passion, and its poverty. Salud to the revolucion. To its glorious triumph. And to its even more magnificent tragedy.

Magical Riolism

It was a summer Saturday in 2000. It had been a bad week. Driving home to lunch I was seized by an impulse. I called Bunny on my cellphone. Don't worry, I'm making your sandwich, she said. Hang the sandwich; what about Rio? I said. What about it? she said. How can we occupy the same planet as a city called the River of January and never visit it? I asked. Absolutely, said Bunny...

Jesus Christ stood arms outstretched like a diver about to plunge off the mountain into the sea far below. Or into the embrace of a born-again Magdalene, reincarnated as the most bewitching of cities. Or maybe Jesus had his arms out to facilitate frisking by a mugger. For after all, this was Rio, equally notorious for its petty street crime as for its seductive charm. To neither of which are even messiahs impervious, leave alone far from invincible travellers like me. Did he suffer the ultimate mugging to save us from such sins? I wondered as I stood at the feet of the giant Christ.

They had all warned me about Rio. The guidebooks, acquaintances who had visited the city, even my travel agent in Delhi. Rio de Janeiro, River of January, Brazil's largest city whose site was first 'discovered' by a Portuguese seaman called Gaspar de Lemos in January 1502, is today billed as one of the world's most unsafe places for the unwary tourist. The visitor is enjoined constantly to repeat the universal catechism of the wayfarer to guard his personal belongings: wallet, watch, spectacles, testicles.

Leave everything of value safely in your hotel room, I had been told repeatedly. Watch, wallet, anything detachable.

Take taxis wherever you go. And if you must walk, carry a couple of bucks on you. For if you are mugged, and the mugger finds absolutely nothing on you, he might relieve you of your family jewels for wasting his time.

Watch, wallet, spectacles ... I intoned under my breath. Stop muttering and look at the view, said Bunny. We were on top of Corcovado, the so-called 'Hunchback' peak which crouches 710 metres above the bay where Copacabana beach curves like the smile of a street-side Madonna. On the mountain stands the cruciform figure of Christ the Redeemer, arguably the most photographed artefact in the southern hemisphere. The thirty-metre, 1000-ton statue, designed by a French sculptor, was to have been installed in 1922, the centenary of Brazil's independence from Portugal, but was finally completed in 1931, after a little financial help from the Vatican.

Camera shutters clicked the Esperanto of a dozen tourist nationalities. Across the panorama of the bay, the outcrop of Pao de Acucar, the Sugar Loaf, thrust out of the sea with phallic emphasis. From here, the River of January seemed like a concrete flood pouring through the lush vegetation of the hillside to reach the sea. Rio's social geography is determined by proximity to the ocean; the rich live closest to the water and the poor are left stranded on the hillsides in favelas, shanty town clusters that scab the upper slopes and reportedly are the source of drugs and street crime. Wallet, watch, I whispered. But everyone was too enraptured by the view to listen. Including Jesus.

Later, we strolled along Copacabana, one of the world's five most famous beaches. Muscular young men played volleyball. Pneumatic nymphets sported all-revealing 'dental floss' micro-bikinis. Rubber-neckers rubber-necked. Nobody paid any attention to my watch, wallet or me. Probably a ploy to lull my suspicions, I thought. We stopped at a beachfront café and ordered a suco, a delicious combination of fresh fruit juices that residents of Rio, or cariocas as they call themselves, are addicted to.

Like their sucos, the cariocas are an inextricably mixed lot. Though slavery was not abolished in the country till 1888, after several armed uprisings, Brazil seems since to have made up for lost time and its people today represent an appealing blend of race and culture. Glass ceilings obviously exist, icons like Pele notwithstanding. But in everyday encounter, carioca society seems cheerfully intermingled, borrowing skin tone and speech cadence from three continents. That's what made it so difficult to identify an obvious minority who could be a mugger, I warned myself. But Bunny was already leading the way to the cable car that would take us to the top of the 400-metre-high Sugar Loaf, which, if anything, gives you an even more spectacular view of Rio than Corcovado does.

As twilight dimmed to dusk, Copacabana and Botafogo beaches cloaked themselves in jewelled light, scintillant sequins on a negligent gown, to tempt the sight of a saint. From his hermit hilltop far above, Christ seemed illumined by their dazzling glow, arms outspread in benediction or surrender. Or perhaps both together. A Carnaval tribute to the Word made pagan flesh to be made Word again. Gaad, isn't this sumthin, twanged an American voice in my ear, shattering the spell like a spiritual mugger.

Let's go, said Bunny. And we went down into the sparkling glitter of the city to sip caipirinhas made of cane spirit, lime juice, sugar and sheer alchemy in a waterfront bar and walked along the beach till Bunny asked me what the time was and I replied that it was past one-thirty in the morning, and said it without realizing that I'd looked at my watch. If not at my wallet, spectacles, etc. What the hell. It was probably too late for muggers anyway.

My un-mugged state was beginning to bother me. If everyone who went to Rio got mugged, why not me? What was the matter with me? Did I look too obviously hard up for even the most desperate of muggers to bother with? We went to Maracana soccer stadium, the biggest in the world with a seating capacity of 180,000, where the national passion of football is celebrated with the full panoply and oompah-pah-pah of war conducted by other means. Mass adrenaline flowed faster than the beer. The crowd roared with jubilation as the home team scored to equalize against Uruguay: one all. The carioca next to me lifted his little son and twirled him around his head like an ecstatically squealing whirligig. No one tried to lift me or my wallet.

On our last night in Rio we took in a samba show. Together with soccer, from which it is sometimes indistinguishable in its nimble legerdemain, samba is a Brazilian speciality. Its most spectacular demonstration is during Carnaval, Rio's annual mega binge. For out-of-season visitors like us, nightclub samba shows are the best substitute. The dancers coruscated across the stage like acrobatic kaleidoscopes, the men sheathed in a sheen of muscle and the women plumed with ribbons and feathers, birds of an earthly paradise. They swept the audience into the dance and I found myself foot-stepping with a towering mulatto, who vanished in the dizzying swirl to be replaced by someone more my size who, it took me a moment to realize, was Bunny. Hola! she said. Hola yourself, I replied. And checking Bunny, watch, wallet, etc., got us out of there before we quite lost our heads.

In the taxi to the airport, I turned for a farewell glimpse of Corcovado. I suddenly felt something missing and clutched at my jacket pocket. Don't tell me your wallet's gone! exclaimed Bunny. Worse, I replied. High on his eyrie, Christ showed his open empty palms. But I knew that Rio, eternal seductress, had forever stolen my heart away.

Last Tango in Buenos Aires

... Don't hang up, I said. If we're going to Rio, what about Buenos Aires as well, City of Beautiful Breezes? City of Beautiful Breezes sounds great to me, senor, said Bunny.

It was only after I had eaten my sandwich that she asked: Were you serious? About going?

Never more so in my life, I replied. So we went.

They are dancing in the streets of Buenos Aires. And what can the dance be but the tango, that sensual and sublime intertwining of love and death. The tango is Argentina's living erotic sculpture, emblem of its mythos of passion and mortality. In a cobble-stoned square in San Telmo, Bunny and I watch Argentina dance to the music of its history, earthy and elegiac.

The man, in ruffled shirt and black trousers, is imperious, demanding. The woman, skin-tight dress slit up the thigh, is yielding, willing to be wooed and won. A nasal accordion insinuates the tango's four-five beat and the dancers begin to move through their predestined steps of courtship, seduction, climax, and oblivion. Ta, ra, ra, ra, Ta, ra, ra, ra, ra ... In out, in out, and roundabout. Spin her, spin out, arms out straight. Hold her, bend her, face to face. Hold her, lift her, legs entwined.

The music pulses faster and faster towards the paroxysm of release thrusting the dancers against each other with exquisitely controlled abandon. Sudden orgasmic crescendo and heartbeat stop. The woman is bent back like a broken rose in the arms of her partner who rears above her, his face a mask of triumphant anguish, the lover who by the act of possessing his beloved must lose her forever.

It takes two to tango, and the two are love and death, I remark, dropping a couple of pesos into the hat the dancers are passing around among the spectators. It gave me goosebumps, says Bunny, getting to the truth of it more succinctly. The story of Argentina—which really means that of Buenos Aires, which comprises over 25 per cent of the country's population of thirty-two million—is enough to give goosebumps to most. What strikes the visitor first about Buenos Aires, city of Good Breezes, is the decidedly European character of both its population and its architecture, epitomized by the resplendent Teatro Colon, home of some of the world's best opera and ballet. The portenas, as residents of Buenos Aires are called, all look European. Unlike in Rio, there are few, if any, signs of an indigenous population, of the hunter-gatherer Indians who were there in 1536 when the Spanish mariner Pedro de Mendoza set up camp at a place he christened 'Puerto Nuestra Senora Santa Maria del Buen Aire'. So what happened to the aboriginal people? The obvious and inevitable inference is that they simply vanished. Much like the supposed political dissidents, centuries later, who 'disappeared' during the so-called 'Dirty War' of 1976–83. Every Thursday afternoon, the mothers of the victims still march in mourning around the central Plaza de Mayo, their vigil a testimony to the elusive mysteries of love and death.

The portena's love of death is nowhere more ostentatiously evident than in Recoleta cemetery. If you belong to the rich and snooty of Argentina, you would not be caught dead in any graveyard other than Recoleta. With its palatial tombs of marble and granite, Recoleta is a virtual necropolis, a city of the dead, whose most prominent resident is Eva Peron, wife of the late military dictator, Juan Peron. Immortalized in Argentine folklore as 'Santa Evita', Eva found her final resting place after a prolonged danse macabre in which her body was 'kidnapped' by political rivals and spirited from South America to Italy, on to Spain and back to Argentina. Her presence—in the family vault of Duarte, her maiden name—is believed to be a matter of literally grave disquiet to her aristocratic neighbours who feel that her plebeian proximity brings down the tone of the place.

When Bunny and I pay our respects to Evita, a fine rain is falling, unmindful of her plea that Argentina not cry for her. It's an embarrassingly trite stage effect. But one which Santa Evita, with her knack of turning cliché into compelling spectacle, would have approved of as an apt tribute from the meteorological department. If not from the production manager Himself.

Death is one of Argentina's most popular pastimes, its success ensured by that other great portena passion: the prodigious ingestion of coronary-inducing red meat. Argentina's vast estancias, or cattle ranches, have made beef and its consumption a pivotal industry. The fashionable pedestrian-only thoroughfares of Florida and Lavalle that crisscross in central Buenos Aires are lined with parrillas, barbeque restaurants, whose plate-glass windows display entire carcasses of beef being char-grilled to perfection on spits. A veggie nightmare and a non-veggie dream come true.

The average portena puts away enough cholesterol-rich meat daily to stop a sabre-tooth tiger dead in its tracks with a heart attack. Offering up a brief mental prayer to Maneka Gandhi to forgive us our politically incorrect trespass, we go to La Estancia, billed as one of the oldest and best parrillas in Buenos Aires. An affable white-jacketed waiter greets us in Portuguese, mistaking us for visiting Brazilians. Non-Portuguese; Indianos, corrects Bunny. Ah, Indianos! Mahatma Gandhi! Beams the waiter delightedly, plonking on the table two huge steaks and a bottle of excellent Argentine wine with a double-handed largesse that would have made poor Bapu blanch with horror.

We really oughtn't to be doing this, you know; apart from everything else it's terribly unhealthy, I remark, digging into my steak, by far the most succulent I've ever eaten. The natives eat like this all the time, and they look fine to me, Bunny replies, looking around at the roomful of diligent carnivores. The difference is, I don't tango; they do, I point out.

And sure enough, when we leave the restaurant to stroll back to the hotel, the dancers are on the street again. The man and the woman are long past their youth. But as they embrace, and part, and embrace again they recreate, through the cadence of their dance, the longing and loneliness of lovers through the ages. In the night sky above, the unfamiliar southern constellations seem to turn and spin with their steps. It suddenly occurs to me that we've never been so far from home. I mention this, and Bunny agrees. Such a long journey; how did we come this far? she murmurs. By Varig airlines, I reply, though both she and I know that's not what we're talking about. We walk away, and as the music fades along deserted Lavalle our footsteps sound an insistent refrain which echoes the twin themes of the tango. Of love and death, and of the distance that joins them, full of endless possibility.